KB212758

Prayer

Prayer *-Letting Go*
by Ven. Pomnyun Sunim

JUNGTO Publishing
1585-16, Seocho-3dong, Seoul, South Korea / +82-2-587-8991

Website : book.jungto.org
e-mail : jungtobook@gmail.com

Printed in South Korea
Third Edition : Winter, 2019

ISBN 978-89-85961-84-4 03220

Prayer
- Letting Go

By Ven. Pomnyun Sunim

JUNGTO

Note : The verses from Dhammapada Sutra that appear at the beginning of the chapters have been cited with the permission from Deep Spring Publisher (Dhammapada, editing / translation by Ven.Guhae Sunim, 2003,). Twenty-three verses have been cited in Chapters 1-21, 26 and 27.

Letting go of ego
Letting go of possessions
Letting go of obstinacy

Contents

III. One Hour of Happiness

IV. Letting Go

For All Those Who Pray

Every day, I meet people who complain that they are unhappy and that their personal relationships are in trouble. They blame others for their problems and suffering. They look outside to find the causes and the solutions to their problems. I always tell them "Suffering originates from ignorance. Look inside your mind. Then, you will find the solution." The attempt to "turn one's eyes inward" is prayer. I say to all those who seek my advice about prayer, "Just pray. Don't worry about whether or not the prayer will be answered."

Some prayers bring happiness while others invite misfortune. Therefore, having a prayer answered is not always a good thing. When praying, it is not important whether or not our objectives are achieved. We should just pray and always be thankful. In other words, since we pray to let go of all attachments in our minds, any outcome is the fulfillment of our prayers.

I wrote this book in the hopes of breaking the stereotypical notion that we pray to fulfill our wishes. I sincerely hope that more people, regardless of their religion, make prayer a part of their lives.

Summer, 2014

Pomnyun

I. The Power of Prayer

01

Praying for the Fulfillment of Wishes

Those who accept a lie as the truth
And regard the truth as a lie
Are trapped in their own incorrect perceptions
And can never attain truth.

First, let's closely examine the meaning of the word, "prayer." Generally speaking, when people say "prayer," they are talking about praying in order to fulfill their wishes. According to the dictionary definition, "Prayer is the act or ritual of making a wish to an absolute being whose capabilities are beyond those of humans." Thus, achieving what we want by borrowing the superior power of a higher being is the general meaning of "prayer."

People use the phrase "inspirational place of prayer" when referring to a place where their fervent prayers have been answered. It is named that way because people believe their prayers will be answered if they go there and pray with all their hearts. This kind of prayer is practiced not only in Buddhism but also in other religious traditions. Futhermore, there are many people whose wishes have come true by praying this way. When someone talks about such an experience, our interest is piqued and we think, "I would also like to have my wishes fulfilled that way." Having our prayers answered this way actually means achieving what we want.

However, does everything we wish for always come true in our lives? Certainly not. As a result, people are happy when their desires are fulfilled and distressed when they aren' t. They may feel like they are in Heaven when their wishes come true but in Hell when they don' t. Depending on whether or not our desires are granted, we drift between pleasure and pain, happiness and despair, and Heaven and Hell, in the course of our lives. This is what we call reincarnation or Samsara[1] in the Buddhist tradition. Unfortunately, trapped inside Samsara, the perpetual cycle of life and death, we pursue a temporary and inauthentic happiness.

---

1. The endless cycle of birth, death and rebirth

02

Going Beyond Reincarnation and Past Life

Just as a tightly woven roof
Will not allow the rain to seep in,
The mind of a diligent practitioner
Will not allow greed and desire to creep in.

What do the teachings of the Buddha actually tell us? The Buddha said both pleasure and anguish are suffering. As long as we are trapped in the cycle of happiness and despair, we cannot fundamentally be free from suffering. Even if we are currently experiencing happiness, it will inevitably turn into sorrow. This is why the Buddha said life is suffering. Furthermore, the Buddha said we need to free ourselves from the chain of reincarnation and from being bound by pleasure and pain. This is called liberation and Nirvana[2].

How, then, can we release ourselves from these bondages of Samsara, the condition of being bound to pleasure and anguish?

To become liberated we must first rid ourselves of desire, which is the cause of both happiness and misery. We must change our belief, "We will be happy only if we achieve what we have been yearning for." This is not to say that we should not have any wishes in the first place. We all have things we hope for, but we should know that sometimes our wishes come true, and other times they do not. By the same token, we should also know that obtaining what we want is not always a good thing, while being unable to achieve something is not necessarily bad. This

---

2. Highest state that someone can attain, a state in which an individual's desires and sufferings are extinguished.

becomes clear if we observe the "law of cause and effect[3]," one of the Buddha's quintessential teachings.

However, most people do not believe they need to understand the laws of nature or make the necessary effort to achieve something. Instead, they blindly pray with the thought, "I will get what I want if I pray hard." This behavior is foolish. This kind of prayer is not in line with the "law of cause and effect."

Furthermore, when people pray, they normally do not have noble aspirations[4] such as turning this world into a "better place" or attaining Enlightenment. They simply want their personal wishes to come true. That is not an altruistic pursuit. Having a noble aspiration means first, letting go of personal greed and stubbornness, followed by setting a worthy goal, and

---

3. Principle that states every result has a cause and that everything happens for a reason.
4. A term used to describe unshakable will and determination to achieve something in the Buddhist tradition.

finally working hard to achieve it. It also means seeking Enlightenment in order to make the world a better place where everyone can be happy.

Therefore, a prayer that is not based on the laws of nature and aims to only fulfill personal desires without effort goes against the teachings of the Buddha. It is neither the way to attain Nirvana nor the way to liberate ourselves from all suffering.

03

Heartfelt Prayer Free from Greed

Do not let your mind get distracted.
Do not indulge in sensual pleasures.
Cultivate the ability to focus your mind
Upon all things that arise and disappear,
Then, You will ultimately awaken to incomparable happiness.

What kind of prayer leads to the path of liberation and Nirvana? Although we call it "prayer," it is actually "practice." "Practice" means "cultivating one's actions." However, since actions originate from the mind, the term actually refers to "cultivating one's mind."

When we refer to a "praying mind" we are talking about a mind that is reverent. We are not talking about a mind that is interested only in satisfying greed. In fact, it is a mind that deeply reflects on past actions, realizing, "I was overly greedy" or "I was trapped in my own thoughts." In short, a praying mind is one that is self-reflective, repents wrong-doings, and is careful not to make the same mistakes again. Traditionally, people first cleansed their bodies and minds before praying. They were cautious with every move they made. For example, they bathed themselves, changed into clean clothes, avoided certain foods, and abstained from sexual activities. They were also careful to keep their minds pure so that they would not become greedy or angry.

Gandhi, India's national movement leader, would go down to his basement alone and quietly fast whenever he became too distracted to work. He fasted for a week to ten days and refused to see anyone. If we meditate while fasting, as Gandhi did, everything we desire out of greed, anger and ignorance will diminish. Then the things we must do will become obvious. We can then focus on these things.

These are what we call "aspirations." Such aspirations are unshakable under any circumstances. The stronger the aspiration the more we need to contemplate, repent, and move forward with devotion. This is true prayer and practice.

When praying, we should not be self-centered and ask, "Please do something for me." If we let go of greed and pray with a clear mind and wisdom, our prayers will be answered. As a matter of fact, our aspirations will be realized more easily and quickly when we perceive things as they are and align our efforts with the law of cause and effect. We should not wish for a stroke of luck or rely on someone else's ability to realize our own aspirations.

The same principle applies to our daily life as well. When someone pesters us for help, we usually assist them but rather reluctantly. For instance, when beggars ask for money, we tend to give them a token amount. However, when we observe people really putting forth an effort, we feel motivated to help them out as much as we can. We don't provide a mere pittance as we do to a beggar. It is the same with praying. Please, don't pray like a beggar. Instead, establish a high aspiration and then cultivate your mind in order to realize it. Ideally, this is how we should pray.

04

In Search of a Path to Healing and Happiness

Do not judge whether someone's behavior is good or bad.
Only reflect on whether your own behavior is good or bad.

In the course of our lives, we suffer from various problems. We say we are unhappy because of our children, parents, spouses, siblings, relatives or friends. We also believe that those close to us hinder us. As a result, we want to become free from such suffering and limitations. Not only do devoted practitioners seek to attain Enlightenment, but also every living creature yearns to escape affliction and restriction.

However, in reality, most of us are bound by them.

To be free from suffering and constraints, we first need to discover the cause. Generally speaking, people blame others for their own misery by insisting that they married the wrong person, their children are disappointing them, their parents aren't capable or their friends annoy them. Also, they may attribute their suffering to a bad job, a low social status, no inheritance or no degree from a prestigious university. Therefore, they believe they need to have better spouses, children, parents, or friends in order to avoid suffering and find happiness. As a result, they spend their entire lives aimlessly searching for people, wealth, fame and power. Ironically, their suffering arises from their desire to obtain these things.

Nothing in this world can be obtained without effort. Because we all think differently, things cannot always go our way, and our thoughts cannot always be right. However, we want to easily fulfill our desires without putting forth the necessary effort. We want things to turn out the way we want and insist that our views are correct.

Our suffering and constraints are not caused by other people or things, but solely by our own perception. The Heart Sutra[5] calls this Chun-Do-Mong-Sang, which literally means a "dream-like, inverted reality" a state in which thoughts are muddled as if in a dream. Unfortunately, this type of inaccurate perception leads to all sorts of suffering and limitations.

Practice is not about praying to get what we want from almighty God or the Buddha. It is about correcting our incorrect perception and acting in accordance with laws of nature. This way, we become free from suffering and constraints, and as a result we can

---

5. Regarded as the summation of the wisdom of the Buddha, the sutra explains the concept of nonattachment and emptiness.

attaining true freedom and happiness.

The Buddha's teachings do not tell us how we should or should not live our lives. They teach us that all actions yield certain consequences. Thus, the teachings help us realize that we must act in a way that enables us to obtain the result we want, and we should avoid certain actions if we don't want the corresponding results. This is the principle of causes, conditions and effects.

Whatever is happening to us now is the result of the causes and conditions we have created for ourselves in the past. Thus, rather than rejecting the consequences or feeling unjustly treated, we should willingly accept them because we know that we have brought them onto ourselves. Also, we must put diligent effort into solving our problems. If we don't like the consequences, we should avoid creating the causes and conditions that will, yet again, yield the same results. Once we know this principle, we can obtain true freedom and happiness regardless of the hardships we face. This is the reason that we need to practice with a clear understanding of the principle of causes, conditions and effects.

05

How to Cultivate the Mind

As a farmer builds waterways for his rice fields,
As a fletcher straightens a curved arrow,
As a carpenter makes a wheel with a piece of wood,
A wise person cultivates his own mind.

We practice to cultivate our minds. All suffering comes from a delusive and ignorant mind. Letting go of such delusions and ignorance and living with a clear mind is called "cultivating the mind." This does not mean the mind has a form or substance we can manipulate. Rather, it means we should let go of our rigid opinions and avoid being controlled by our ignorance and delusions.

Sometimes, we have dreams while sleeping. Dreams, which come from our subconscious, seem quite real while we are in them. After waking up, we realize it was just a dream, but we are not aware of it while we are dreaming. We run away from a robber in our dreams because we are scared, and we are grateful if someone rescues us. Once awake, however, we realize that neither the assailant who frightened us nor the hero who saved us exists in reality. We were simply caught up in a dream. We no longer suffer if we wake up from such delusions. Buddhist practice addresses this principle.

There are many different kinds of Buddhist practices for cultivating the mind: Vipassana meditation[6] in Southern or Theravada Buddhism[7]; Hwadu[8] meditation in Zen Buddhism[9]; chanting,

---

6. Widely practiced in Theravada Buddhism, it uses mindfulness to note every detail of our mental and physical experience from moment-to-moment, with an unbiased attitude.

reciting mantra, studying sacred texts and repentance in Mahayana Buddhism[10]. Among these various practices, I will talk about "repentance practice."

Repentance means feeling remorse for past transgressions and, at the same time, vowing to avoid repeating the same mistakes in the future. Furthermore, repentance requires fully accepting the consequences of the causes and conditions that we have created rather than blaming others for our current situation. In other words, we should accept what happens to us as the result of our own actions with the thought, "This

---

7. A conservative branch of Buddhism mostly practiced in Sri Lanka, Myanmar, Thailand, Laos, and Cambodia.

8. It means "keyword" or "word-head." It refers to specific words or short questions used to meditation such as" "Who am I?" or "What is this?" Hwadu meditation is used extensively in Korean Buddhism.

9. An outgrowth of Mahayana Buddhism practiced in some parts of China and Japan that focuses on meditation.

10. A liberal branch of Buddhism practiced in Tibet, China, Korea, and Japan, which seeks Enlightenment not only for themselves but for all sentient beings.

is the consequence of my wrongdoing." We should also guard against creating causes and conditions that lead to negative karmic results. Thus, we should refrain from saying certain things or taking certain actions if we don't want the result they will bring. To reiterate, repentance practice is willingly accepting the outcome of the causes and conditions that we have created and vowing never to repeat them.

06

How to Control Anger

Just as a large boulder on the mountain
Is unshaken by the wind,
A wise person
Is unmoved by either praise or insult.

Let's carefully examine the suffering in our minds. We realize we often get angry. We get angry because our children watch TV instead of doing their homework after school. We get angry when our husbands come home drunk late at night. We get angry when our wives go out too often, neglecting the children. We get angry when our parents nag at us. We also become angry when a trusted friend doesn't pay back the money he borrowed.

But let's look at the situation from a different angle. Why did we get angry? It was because we could not understand the other person. We get frustrated and upset when we don't have a clue why our children don't do their homework, why our husbands get drunk and come home late, why our wives go out so often, why our parents nag or why a friend won't pay us back. They don't make us angry ; we get angry because we cannot understand them.

So, why can't we understand them? It's because we see things only from our own point of view. We want others to appreciate our perspective while we make no effort to comprehend theirs. We instead demand, "You should try to understand how I feel." When we say, "I don't know why on earth you would do that," we are actually saying, "I don't want to understand you," and, "I really have no desire to try to understand you." What happens to us when we talk like this? We feel pressure in our chest ; the irritation in our voice grows ; our face tightens ; and we can't sleep. These are the signs of suffering.

What, then, can we do in order to alleviate our suffering? Will we find happiness when everyone understands us, when our children study hard, when our husbands come home early, when our wives don't go out, when our parents stop nagging, and when our friend pays back our money?

If that were the case, it would mean other people have the power to control our happiness or suffering. We are joyful or miserable depending on what others say or do. Can people who lead such lives be considered to have full ownership of their lives? No, these people's lives are not their own. They are completely subject to the words and actions of others.

Let's try to see things from other people's perspective. For example, "You were just watching TV after coming home because something bad happened to you at school. You drank because you were stressed out at work. So that's why you went out so much! You couldn't pay me back because of that reason." If we try to understand and accept others by saying, "Oh, that's why…," we will calm down, and our suffering will disappear. Our strained expressions will relax, and our voices will become softer. We will become more free and happy. Someone else's actions and words will no longer have undue influence over our lives. As soon as we understand other people's perspectives and think, "Oh, that's why they smiled." or "Oh, that's why they frowned." we will not be affected by either their smiles or their frowns.

When we are able to reflect ourselves and say, "I never knew that!" or "Wow, I completely misunderstood that!" our deepseated hard feelings will melt away. Our burdened and clouded minds will then become light and clear. This is what we call "repentance."

07

Keeping Your Mind and Body Humble

A wise person
Listens attentively to the Dharma
And maintains his mind serene
Like a deep, clear and calm lake.

When two people lying on their backs find their opinions differ and begin to argue because each thinks he is right, they abruptly get up without realizing it. If they were sitting down, they would stand up, and if they were standing, they would raise their heads and glare at each other. On the other hand, if they realize, "I misunderstood," or "I was wrong." they lower their heads, curve their rigid backs, kneel, and move their entire body to bow down.

That's why we do prostrations when we pray in repentance.

Just as the body lowers when the mind becomes humble, so the mind also acquiesces once the body is lowered. Repentance begins in the mind. When there is a change in the mind, the body follows suit. Since actions arise from the mind, refining our actions equates to cultivating our mind. When we do prostrations, we realize in our hearts, "I'm really inadequate." and "I've made some bad mistakes."

Once we begin to realize, "Oh my goodness, I've done a terrible thing!" all of our resentment completely disappears, and we naturally lower our heads. Some may ask, "Isn't it enough to humble our minds? Do we really have to go so far as to actually do prostrations?" They are not necessarily wrong. However, when our minds become humble, our bodies naturally assume humble postures as well. So what these people are actually saying is that they do not wish to humble their minds.

"I got angry at my child yesterday. I yelled at her because I was too attached to my thoughts and did not take her feelings into account. I am so sorry, darling." "Yesterday, I got irritated and angry with my husband. After calming down and thinking things through, however, I realized that I simply failed to understand that there are times when he'll come home late after having a drink with coworkers. When my husband saw that I was angry, he actually tried to calm me down by apologizing for drinking and coming home late. I was self-righteous and was only concerned about being right and proving him wrong. I've been so foolish." This is how we should reflect upon our everyday behavior as we do prostrations. With every single prostration we should repent, "I've been foolish." "I failed to understand my husband's feelings." "I didn't understand my wife's feelings."

"She probably feels confined staying at home all day long." This is how we become more understanding of others.

We should repent that we have failed to understand our spouses and that we have resented them. Only then can we be truly free. We can be happy regardless of another person's words or actions. But in order to be free and happy, we need to pray every day, reflecting upon and repenting the things we did the day before.

08

Reasons for Doing Daily Prayer

Overcoming oneself
Is truly better than overcoming others.
Therefore, if you discipline your mind,
You will gain freedom in all your actions.

Resolving deeply rooted hard feelings in one's mind during repentance prayers is called "extinguishing karmic hindrances[11]." Merely doing prostrations, by repeatedly lowering the body down to the ground and raising it back up, does not automatically extinguish karmic hindrances. These deeply rooted hard

---

11. Refers to the obstacles in life sentient beings created themselves due to their ignorance, greed and temperaments.

feelings can be extinguished by sincere reflection through repentance prayer.

In addition to self reflection, pledging, "Even if someone's behavior rubs me the wrong way, I won't get caught up in my own thoughts and react rashly as I usually do," helps us guard against future wrong-doings. If we practice repentance prayer daily, we won't get as resentful as we used to. Also, we won't cry over the things that used to make us cry. Even if we were to lose our temper, we wouldn't feel miserable about it all day long. Instead, we would repent right way, realizing, "I was trapped in my own thoughts again." Thus, as suffering and the restrictions diminish, freedom and happiness will expand in our lives. This is the reason we pray every day.

However, just because someone doesn't pray in repentance every day, we cannot say, "This person does not practice." Being mindful of our reactions to different situations at every moment is practice and prayer in themselves.

The lives of farmers illustrate this point. Chopping wood and plowing fields are good exercises for farmers. That's why they stay healthy even without engaging in any particular exercise regimen. On the other hand, as city dwellers, we often become ill due to the lack of physical activity in our daily lives. So we usually need to have on an exercise routine and work out regularly at a designated time. Of course there's little need to take time out for a particular exercise regimen if, in a normal day, we were to walk long distances instead of driving everywhere, or run up and down the stairs instead of always taking the elevator. It's difficult, however, to consistently exercise, so we must set aside some time for physical exercise. Only with regular exercise routine can we keep healthy.

Similarly, we may believe it's easy to repent and look inward when facing challenges, but in reality, it's not that easy. Doing repentance prayer daily at a set time not only extinguishes our accumulated karmic hindrances but also gives us inner strength to reflect on ourselves in our everyday lives. Needless to say, it is imperative for practitioners to select a certain time of the day and pray consistently.

09

A Clear Understanding of Your karma

A person who does not seek learning
Is no different from an aging bull.
He only gains in weight,
But not in wisdom.

What, exactly, is the right way to practice?

You must first identify your deep-seated mental and emotional barriers, commonly referred to as "karmic hindrances" in the Buddhist tradition. For example, a mother, troubled by a child who neither listens to her nor does homework, may resort to praying, "Please, let everything turn out well for my child." But praying for everything to go well doesn't mean it will. We, instead, need to examine the reasons the child is disobedient and doesn't do homework. After observing the situation, we find that the mother expects a great deal from her child. Dissatisfaction with her husband, which has accumulated after years of unmet expectations, is redirected toward her child onto whom she pins all of her hopes. As a result, the mother's unrealistic expectation is placed on the child and he ends up resenting his mother as the burden becomes unbearable.

At that point, the mother should begin prayer of repentance toward her husband. Practicing repentance prayer will make her discontentment with her husband disappear as her expectations become more realistic. As a result, her dissatisfaction with her child will naturally vanish. Then, as the mother's complaints about the child subside, the child's resentment toward the mother will, likewise, melt away.

As this case exemplifies, we need to discover the root cause of the suffering buried within us. As we learn to identify fundamental sources of emotional suffering and root them out from our minds, all other entwined knots will effortlessly unravel themselves. In other words, if we can identify our emotional scars and begin to let them go, we may even heal the ones we were not conscious of. As a result, the remaining problems that arise from these wounds will naturally disappear. That is why we need to understand our core issues and focus on resolving them. This process is called, "the extinction of karmic hindrance".

Some people, for example, harbor deep resentment toward their parents who did not raise them with care or provide them with a good education. People who have unmet expectations because of their parents tend to look to their spouses to satisfy their unfulfilled needs. They inevitably become dissatisfied with their spouses when their needs remain unmet and subsequently transfer their hopes onto their children. However, the mothers are again left frustrated and disappointed when their children fail to satisfy the high expectations they placed on them. On the surface, the problem may seem like one between parents and children, but if we take a deeper look, it is a problem between spouses. Probing even deeper, however, we can see that the problem actually originated from their relationship with their parents. Upon this realization, they should practice repentance toward their parents. Only then will their deeply ingrained resentment melt away.

In this manner, we need to identify the source of our suffering and practice prayers of repentance in order to heal ourselves. It is important for each of us to look into the very depths of our hearts in order to figure out what kinds of anxieties and resentments we have, and then offer prayers of repentance to free ourselves from these negative emotions.

Mental and emotional barriers, also known as karma[12], are embedded deeply in our minds and subconsciously control what we say, do and think. This is why we experience amazing changes in our lives once we become aware of our deepest emotional wounds and focus on healing them with prayers of repentance. First of all, we become more peaceful. As we gain a better understanding of ourselves, we become more tolerant of other people's behavior. And once our relationship troubles with others evaporate, the whole world seems like a more beautiful place. This is the path to Nirvana and Enlightenment.

We dislike and resent other people because we are oblivious to the causes and conditions we ourselves have created. We feel offended and angry when we only perceive the consequences. Once we become aware of the causes and conditions that we have created, our anger and resentment will vanish. When

---

12. Habitual perception that dictates one's thoughts, speech and actions.

we practice repentance prayer, we become more confident because our inner strength grows. Happiness is not about avoiding sickness, having everything go according to plan or being praised by others. As long as we practice being mindful of the causes and conditions that we have created, we can attain Enlightenment even if we become sick, experience failure, or receive criticism from others. Therein lies the path to freedom and happiness.

10

The Sweet Temptation that Hinders Prayer - Majang

Come and see the world.
The world is like an ornate royal carriage
Where the foolish struggle inside.
But the wise do not become attached to it.

Even though we know what prayer is, how to pray, and how to control our minds, we do not automatically become free from the hindrances of our past karma. We often face obstacles called "Majang"[13] when we engage in practice. Even though the literal meaning of Majang in Buddhist practice is "obstruc-

---

13. Korean term for Mara, which means temptation that hinders practice.

tion of the devil," it does not mean there is an actual evil entity that hinders our prayers. Instead, Majang manifests itself in various forms, such as delusions, misconceptions or distracting thoughts. Among these, past misconceptions and foolish ideas, which we thought we had discarded, are so deeply rooted within our subconscious minds that they often re-surface to haunt us.

Here is an example. A woman was unhappy because her husband would often drink and come home late. She tried in vain to put an end to her husband's drinking by seeking the advice of fortune-tellers, hiring a shaman to perform various rituals, and even praying fervently, but nothing helped. Her efforts to stop her husband's drinking habit came from her firm belief that she was right and her husband's behavior was wrong. Since she believed that her husband's drinking was bad and had to be stopped, in her mind, her thoughts and actions were justified. She was, therefore, only concerned with finding a good method of putting an end to her husband's drinking.

Practicing, on the other hand, gives her an opportunity to reflect upon herself instead of pinning the blame on her husband as the source of the problem. The belief that her husband's drinking is a problem was based on her own view that alcohol is bad. Is her assumption correct? If not, is alcohol good? That's not true either. In fact, alcohol is neither inherently good nor bad. This concept in Buddhism is known as "emptiness" [14], which is the "true nature of all existence." The woman failed to see the true nature of alcohol and was blinded by the belief that alcohol is bad. As a result, she thought it was wrong for her husband to drink and resented him for it. Her

---

14. A quintessential teaching of Buddhism that states no individual person or thing has any permanent and fixed identify.

way of thinking can be described as "being attached to form," which leads to suffering. If she were to let go of her presupposition that alcohol is bad, her problem would be immediately resolved. Then, her negative image of her drinking husband will also disappear. Her problem will be solved instantly when she realizes that the nature of all existence is "emptiness."

However, despite this realization, she may find herself becoming upset again at the sight of her husband's drinking because her negative reaction toward it has become deeply ingrained in her mind. So, to reprogram her mind, it is important for her to pray each day. During her daily prayer, while doing prostrations, she needs to recite to herself, "Alcohol is a restorative herbal medicine for my husband." Even though this maxim doesn't contain the words "the nature of all things is emptiness," it will, nevertheless, alter her perception that alcohol is bad. In fact, since alcohol is a restorative herbal medicine for her husband, he should drink a lot of it on a regular basis. Now that alcohol is instilled with a positive value, her husband's drinking can no longer be a source of frustration and suffering for her. She will now be happy if he comes home after drinking because he has taken his medicine. If he hasn't had as much as usual, she can fix him another drink. And if he comes home sober, she can mix drinks for him. She will no longer be affected by her husband's drinking, much less by how much he drinks.

Through prayer, she is able to change her views and, as a result, experience peace of mind. Additionally, when she is relaxed, so is her husband. Since she is less sensitive and less likely to get as angry as before, her husband will, of course, feel less stress and have fewer reasons to drink. Initially, she began practicing prayer with the desire to change her husband, but she ended up experiencing a transformation in her own beliefs. This is a positive outcome for both her and her husband. She now comes to realize the potential benefit of practice and the wisdom of the Dharma.

However, while praying consistently, if she happens to notice that her husband begins to drink less or even stops drinking, she may believe that her prayer is working and become overly enthusiastic. Consequently, she may even be motivated to increase the number of her prostrations from 108 to 300. Unfortunately, this is not the right way to pray.

Praying is about altering one's own thoughts. The fact that she became happy because her husband was drinking less is an indication that she reverted back to her original thought of wanting things to turn out the way she desired, to have her husband stop drinking. At first, she was unhappy because things didn't go the way she wanted, and now she is happy because they did. Both her happiness and unhappiness originate from her belief that things must go her way. This is not the right way to pray, because she is still attached to her own thoughts. If she continues to pray while grasping onto her own beliefs, she will begin to think that her husband will stop drinking altogether if she prays harder. This will only reinforce her expectations, and she will inevitably become more disappointed with her husband when things don't turn out the way she wants. She will begin to wonder, "Why won't he stop drinking when I am praying so hard?" and she will become increasingly frustrated. She will then come to the conclusion that "Praying is useless," and eventually stops praying altogether. This is precisely how Majang interferes with practice.

When praying, we must be careful about Majang. Majang is foolish thoughts that arise in our minds. Both being unhappy when things don't go our way and being happy when things do go our way hinder our practice. All of us fall prey to Majang quite easily.

The Buddha overcame many extreme hardships over the course of his six-year ascetic practice. Right before attaining Enlightenment, the Buddha was visited by the Devil King[15] himself who enticed the Buddha with anything he wanted. The Devil King even went so far as to offer the Buddha the position of King of Heaven of Desire, the sweetest of all worldly propositions. It is worthwhile to note here that the offer symbolizes our inner desires rather than external temptations. Just like the Buddha, it is only by overcoming temptations that arise in our minds that we can embark upon the path toward Nirvana.

In short, we believe things should turn out the way we want them to, which is why we become unhappy when they don't. We are in Heaven when we get

---

15. Dwells in the highest or the sixth heaven of the world of desires and obstructs Buddhist practice.

what we want, but we are thrust into Hell when we don't. "Reincarnation" is the process of alternating endlessly between Heaven and Hell because of our desires. If we let go of our desires, both Heaven and Hell will disappear. This is the way to become truly free and attain Enlightenment.

11

Be Dignified, Not Servile
Be Humble, Not Arrogant

Rare is to be born a human being
Rare is to have eternal life
Rare is to hear the true Dharma
Rare is for a Buddha to be born.

Not everyone goes to a Buddhist temple with the high aspiration of becoming a Buddha. Some go to the temple to find relief from their suffering, to attain peace of mind or even to fulfill their desires. They go to a Buddhist temple with hopes of solving their problems related to family, business, health, and so on. However, all problems and sufferings basically stem from the mind.

Our greed is a disease that is caused by the delusion, "It's mine." Also, all our anger and irritation have their roots in the belief, "I am right." Letting go of our sense of ownership, or "It's mine." is called non-possession, and letting go of our stubborn thoughts, or "I'm right." is called non-egocentrism. Once we reach a state of nonpossession and non-egocentrism, we will no longer experience suffering. Even though we are stubborn and live with greed, anger and foolishness, we can enter the path of Enlightenment the moment we let go of these things. We can achieve Buddhahood when we orient our lives toward non-possession and nonegocentrism. When we learn this principle and act accordingly, any one of us can live a life that is free and without suffering regardless of our race, gender, age, religion, education level and whether we lead secular or monastic lives.

We practice because we hope to emulate the way

the Buddha had lived. The Buddha went barefoot, wore threadbare clothes, slept under trees, and ate food that others gave him. He was poorer than anyone in the world but was happier than a king and was so wise that everyone sought his advice about how to live a better life. He was neither lonely when he was alone, nor bothered when he was in a crowd of thousands. For the Buddha, being alone in the woods was good for meditating, and being in a noisy market place was good for imparting his teachings to people.

Having no food was good for focusing on practice, and having plenty of food enabled him to share it with others. Being criticized by people helped him to practice perseverance, while being admired by them made it easy for him to spread the Dharma. Regardless of the circumstances, the Buddha lived a life that was free and without suffering. The very path of Buddhist practice is to emulate the Buddha's life and become like him.

When we attain true freedom and happiness, we won't be servile even if we don't own anything. Also, if we repent because we realize our own shortcomings, we won't be arrogant wherever we may go. Thus, the goal of a practitioner is to live a dignified and humble life that is free of both servility and arrogance.

II. Prayer of a Practitioner

In Ven. Pomnyun Sunim's question-and-answer Dharma talks, many people candidly talk about their personal problems in the hopes of receiving Pomnyun Sumin's prayer guidance that can solve their problems. However, there is no magical mantra that can solve our problems. Directing our vision inward from the outside is our only effective prayer. When we pray this way daily, our suffering and restrictions begin to disappear before we know it.

12

When Prayers Are Not Answered

- How to view what has already happened

Desires give birth to sorrow.
Desires also give birth to fear.
One who is liberated from desires
Has neither sorrow nor fear.

It has been about 50 days since I began the 100-Day Prayer. My son wants to wait a whole year in order to retake the national college entrance exam, and I'm not sure whether I should support him in that decision or persuade him to apply to colleges that he can get accepted into now. I also don't know what to do about my husband who wants to quit his job and start his own business. It seems like both my husband and son are unclear and indecisive about what they want to do, and I don't know

how to help them. Do you think that there is something
wrong with the way I've been praying?

Your problem has nothing to do with prayer. All kinds of things happen in this world whether we pray or not. By the same token, no matter how hard we pray, things that are not meant to happen won't happen. We pray in order to change the way we perceive the events that have already taken place. Specifically, praying helps us accept the reality with a positive attitude instead of agonizing, "Why did this have to happen to me?" An incident that may have been a traumatic experience for a non-practitioner can actually be beneficial for a practitioner.

The questioner says she is praying, but in reality, she's not. The way she relates her problems to prayer shows that she expects things to go well if she prays. But, the happenings in our lives are neither good nor bad. They are simply events that occur. Incidents such as being involved in a car accident, losing a job, or failing an exam are not necessarily negative occurrences. We view them as bad, but they have no inherent value in themselves. What makes events fortunate or unfortunate depends on our perspective. If we don't practice, every time something happens, we're bound to judge the incident as "good" or "bad," which leads to suffering. If we practice, we can find a positive aspect even in what others would normally consider a bad situation.

For example, armed robbers occasionally show up at the JTS (Join Together Society) project site in Dungeshwari, India. We have suffered material losses as a result, and some JTS volunteers have been seriously hurt. On the surface, these are unfortunate incidents, but they also brought positive outcomes. Dungeshwari, which used to be an unsafe place plagued by crime, became a decent place to live when JTS came and revitalized the town. As a result, real estate speculators began to take an interest in the region. Occasional robberies, however, have kept them at bay. On the one hand, these larcenies have caused us the inconvenience of having to guard the place every night in order to prevent more crime.

On the other hand, they have kept outsiders from swarming into the region for indiscriminate real estate speculation. As you can see, the very same incident can take on a drastically different light depending on our perspective. If we view robbery only negatively, it is something that must never happen. However, when we understand that there are positive aspects to every situation, we no longer need to fear anything that may happen to us.

The questioner seems to think it will be the end of the world if her son chooses to retake the college entrance exam, but someone who practices should be able to deal with the situation calmly. After attentively listening to her son's plans, she can either encourage him to apply to the college that will accept him with his current score or allow him to retake the exam the following year, if that is what he wants to do.

Whatever she decides to do will all be absolutely fine. The same is true regarding her husband's situation. In the past, she may have believed that things had to be a certain way for her to be satisfied. Now that she practices, she can openly discuss things with her family members to find ways for everyone to be happy. She may candidly express her opinion if she thinks her husband's business plan is short-sighted or she may decide to support him in his decision. It is more important that each day of our lives be meaningful, free and happy. We need some money and basic education to lead satisfying lives, but money and education are not the most important things in life.

Practitioners do not view things as "good" or "bad" but only see things as they are. With consistent prayer, we learn to view things without bias and seek out solutions by talking with our families whenever problems occur. Slowly but surely, our minds grow stronger and more stable, enabling us to stay calm even when others around us are not. The inner strength we gain from praying is the blessing of the Buddha.

13

When You Want to Be a Strong Support to Your Family

- Whether or not your wishes are fulfilled is unimportant

Give up your anger.
Discard your pride.
Free yourself from all attachments.
Those without attachments to their body and mind
Will not fall into suffering.

My husband's business is in serious trouble. My son was fine until middle school, but he seems to be having a hard time since starting high school. I am physically and mentally exhausted. What kind of prayer can help me cultivate peace of mind?

People want everything to go their way, and they

feel miserable when it doesn't. That's why they seek help from others when they can't do it themselves. And when it's beyond human power, they seek divine intervention to get what they want. Therefore, divine beings must be omniscient and omnipotent, or else they wouldn't be able to satisfy our wishes. When we are extremely anxious, it does help momentarily to pray devoutly to a divine being. This, however, is not practice. The purpose of practice is to realize that not everything in life will be pleasing to us.

Would it actually be good if everything turned out the way we wanted? No, it wouldn't. Let's assume that all the people in the world are able to fulfill their wishes. Would that make the world a Heaven? In truth, the world would immediately become Hell. For example, let's say that two women are attracted to the same man. What would happen if both women got their way? Generally, people want to become rich without working hard and wish to attend prestigious universities without putting in the necessary effort. Imagine what would happen if all their wishes came true?

Everything in this world cannot always go our way. So does that mean nothing ever will? No, that's not true either. Sometimes we get what we want, and other times we don't. More often than not, however, we don't end up with what we want.

If we want to achieve something, we need to be willing to work for it. Putting in the effort does not necessarily mean we will attain our goals. Nevertheless, we need to continue trying. So, what happens when we don't succeed despite our hard work? We need to figure out what went wrong and try again. What if that still doesn't work? We try once more. And what if we fail yet another time? Then, it's alright to give up. What happens if we just don't want to give up? Well, then we can simply try again. This is life.

When we have worked toward a goal and have finally reached it, we are very happy. Should we then stop working? No, we begin to focus on another target. What do we do when we have reached that objective as well? We would then set another goal and begin striving toward it.

Working on goal B after having achieved goal A is virtually the same as working on goal B after failing to achieve goal A. Whether or not we reach a particular result is not really that important. What's most important is how hard we work toward our goal. If we accomplish something as a result of our intense effort, we can move on to another objective. Likewise, if we miss the mark despite our diligence, we can then choose to either continue trying or focus on a different target. It's essentially the same whether we work on something else because we have successfully completed the task or because we have failed at it.

Finally, it doesn't make any difference even if we hold onto the same project despite having failed many times.

If we make ourselves miserable when things don't go our way, we may suffer for the rest of our lives. We are in a constant state of anxiety because things don't turn out the way we want. Consequently, we cling to other people or a divine being who can help us realize our wishes. In reality, however, there is no way we can achieve everything we desire in life.

Just imagine how many students in Korea don't get accepted into the college of their choice and end up spending an extra year or even two years preparing to retake the college entrance exam. Who wouldn't want to attend Seoul National University, the most prestigious university in Korea? But do rejected applicants give up their lives when they don't get in? No, they carry on with their lives.

When your husband has a hard time because his

business is in trouble, you should not think, "How can I help him out with his business?" Instead, you should focus on giving him the emotional support he needs to overcome the crisis. Wanting to help your child so that he can do well on the exam is actually an attempt to fulfill your own wish. Even if he fails on his exam, you should think, "How can I console and encourage my son?"

You need to practice in order to achieve such a state of mind. Even with practice, sometimes you will be successful and other times you will not. Likewise, sometimes your wishes come true and other times they don't. It is more important that you remain calm and stable. With equanimity, you will be able to assist both your husband and child. Instead of worrying and being anxious like the rest of your family, you can be a pillar of strength, giving them encouragement and comfort.

It is not possible to possess this kind of composure

without practice. In order to become such a person, you need to constantly remind yourself, "Thank you, Buddha. Everything is going well and I have no worries." You should pray wholeheartedly to the Buddha with gratitude.

14

When It is Difficult to Repent

- Perceiving things as they are

As an experienced charioteer skillfully controls
the speed of his chariot,
The one who keeps his anger in check as it arises within him,
I call him a true charioteer.

Whenever I listen to your Dharma talks, it seems like you are telling me to pray in repentance toward the people I dislike in order to become free from suffering. But I really don't feel like repenting toward my husband. I can understand why he is the way he is, but I find myself resenting him before I am aware of it. How do I repent toward my husband? Is it OK to pray while I continue to resent him?

When we resent someone, we are actually the ones who suffer. The purpose of repentance prayer is not in becoming an open-minded, well-mannered and sophisticated person. Rather we repent so that our emotional pain can be alleviated.

If you meet 10 people throughout the day and dislike all of them, your life would be Hell. If, on the other hand, you meet 10 people and like all of them, your life would be Heaven. Whether or not your husband smokes, drinks, or comes home late at night is strictly his concern. How miserable you would be if you hated the sun going down, clouds forming in the sky and the rain falling. They are simply natural phenomena. Just as you acknowledge "Ah, the sun is going down!" or "Ah, it's raining!" without resisting the weather, simply accept other people exactly as they are. Then, you won't be unhappy. However, you'll become completely miserable if you try to control your husband by demanding he come home early, refrain from drinking and smoking and never look at other women.

When you have such a perspective, you will inevitably become unhappy. You pray in the hopes that your husband will change, but you end up disappointed with the Buddha for not granting your wish. Neither the Buddha nor God can help you with in this case. The source of the problem is your own lack of wisdom. You don't have to stay in a marriage if you don't get along with your husband. If you really don't love him anymore you can simply say "good-bye" and leave him, but there's no reason to hold a grudge against him. You have the freedom to choose to stay or leave. However, it is unwise to resent your husband. If your intention is to continue to live with your spouse, you should not despise him. If, on the other hand, you plan to leave him, there is still no reason to hate him. You need to understand that your resentment comes from judging your husband only from your own perspective. This insight will enable you to understand why you should not hate your husband.

In reality, however, no matter how hard you try not to resent him, you may not be able to help it. It's the same as craving a cigarette every time you see one even though you want to quit smoking. Just like you can't stand the sight of your husband despite your intentions not to hate him, your husband is also likely to drink when he meets his friends even though he did not meant to.

Similarly, he'd like to come home early, but hanging out with his friends, he somehow ends up staying out all night. He doesn't mean to stare at other women, but when he sees someone attractive he can't help himself. It's easy to recognize when others do foolish things, but it's not so easy to see or control our own foolish behavior. Unfortunately, this is why our lives are full of suffering.

If you want to end this suffering, you must realize that your own habits, not other people, are the cause of your suffering. You are unable to quit smoking because you can't break the habit. It's not the cigarette's fault. Instead of making the excuse that you smoked because your friends were smoking, you need to realize that it was your own habit that impelled you to smoke. Likewise, insisting that you tried not to despise your husband but you couldn't help it because of what he did is also just an excuse. In the end, you have to decide how you'll live your life. If you want to continue feeling contempt for your husband and stay miserable, you are free to do so. However, if you want a happy life, you should accept your husband as he is since he is just living his own life.

Many times, you make promises to yourself but can't keep them. That is the reality. You vowed not to do something because you felt in your conscience that you shouldn't continue doing it, but your old habits prevent you from keeping the promise. How can you expect to make others do what you want when you can't even control yourself? As you become aware of how hard it is to change yourself, you can more readily accept your husband as he is. Then, there will be fewer conflicts between the two of you, making your household more peaceful. Even if you end up leaving your husband, you won't have regrets if the separation is amicable.

If you logically analyze your husband's speech and actions, you will realize that he is simply being himself with no intention of hurting you. He thinks, talks and behaves based on the habits that have been formed since his childhood. Just as there are big trees, small trees and all different kinds of trees in the mountains, there are all kinds of people in the world who perceive, make judgments, think, talk and act in their own individual ways. This applies not only to your husband but to everyone in the world, including you and me. Just say to yourself, "Oh, this is how everyone is…" With this realization, you can stop insisting on your ways and accept your husband just as he is.

You become angry and irritated when you judge others, thinking, "That is not the right way," or "This is wrong," based solely on your habits and self-interests. Thus, before you knew this, you might have said, "It's your fault." But now that you know better, you can acknowledge that such emotions are the manifestation of your own habitual perception, also known as karma. Your hatred is not caused by what other people say or do but rather comes from your disapproving opinions about their behavior. You become angry because you insist something is right or wrong based on your perspective.

When you pray without knowing this principle,

you are likely to pray to the Buddha, "Please change my husband for me." However, once you know, you will be able to reflect back on your actions and realize, "Earlier, we fought because I insisted that I was right." It doesn't mean your husband's behavior is praiseworthy. Instead, it means that becoming irritated or hating him for his actions is actually caused by your perception. Therefore, while doing prostrations, if you can realize and repent, "Oh my, I got caught up in my own thoughts again," you will be able to see your husband in a more positive light. Please keep this principle in mind when doing repentance prayer.

15

When Your Mind Does Not Become Earnest in Prayer

- Sincerely reflecting on yourself

Advancing step by step along the right path,
Moment by moment,
A wise man sheds his emotional afflictions
Like a goldsmith removing impurities from gold.

What is a sincere prayer, one that does not ask or wish for something? Also, when I pray, I can't concentrate because my mind races with all kinds of distracting thoughts. What can I do to pray with deep earnestness?

When do you think a person has an earnest mind? Your prayer will naturally become sincere when your back is against the wall, and you feel you have no way out. If you keep wishing, "I wish I could pray earnestly. When will I be able to have an earnest mind?" you are asking for trouble. You are actually courting disaster if you continue to think that way because a catastrophe must happen for you to fulfill your wish. When there is a crisis in the family such as a family member being diagnosed with cancer or experiencing serious problems, people become desperate and are naturally bound to pray zealously. Therefore, it's best that you don't dwell on such foolish thoughts. Not being able to pray with an earnest mind means you don't have a lot of suffering in your life. Therefore, you should appreciate your present situation.

Don't be swayed when others insist that you should have a religion or be very devout in your faith or that you should perform certain religious rituals. Why would you let others have so much influence over the only life you have? When you experience relationship issues with your spouse or children, or encounter any other problems in your life, you should first try to resolve them on your own. If you're not able to resolve things despite your best efforts, you can then try taking refuge in the Dharma. You may be pleasantly surprised to find that your problems are resolved when you diligently follow the Buddha's teachings. Even then, you shouldn't just pray with wishful thinking, "Good things will happen if I pray." Likewise, you should neither attend a particular church nor go to a certain temple just because someone tells you that your prayer will be answered there.

You must first comprehend the principles behind the Buddha's teachings. For instance, if your child doesn't listen to you, you need to understand that your child's resistance grew out of the seed which you unknowingly planted in him. Within that seed is your defiance against your husband's ways. Understanding this principle will help you realize why you need to pray in repentance toward your husband. Your prayers will naturally become earnest after you come to realize that you must sincerely repent if you wish to resolve the issues with your child. What does it mean to have an earnest mind? It means making prayer your first priority. For instance, if you decide to pray at 5 a.m. you must pray at that time no matter what happens. You also need to always adhere to the goal of your prayer. If, for example, the aim of your prayer is to honor your husband's wishes, you should not argue with him regardless of what he says or does. Because your prayer's objective is your top priority, anything your husband may do – coming home late, drinking or even gambling – all becomes secondary. Your problem can only be solved if you firmly commit and follow through with your prayer.

Most people, however, see no change in their lives despite practicing Buddhism for five or even 10 years because they fail to pray with such total devotion. Only when we make a firm resolve and follow through can we change our lives. A half-hearted attempt will not help us. Complacently hoping to solve your problem with the help of the Buddha is not the right attitude of a Buddhist. We should, instead, devote ourselves to practice and take refuge in the Dharma. We must accept, comprehend, and act upon the Dharma with a fearless determination to free ourselves from ignorance. By taking full responsibility, we can overcome any problem we may face. This is the blessing of the Buddha. Only when our practice is based on true selfreflection, repentance and constant self-awareness, can we experience the benefits of his teachings.

Let's think about our lives. When we are young, we need the help of our parents. But if we continue to ask our parents for help after becoming adults, we will be labeled as irresponsible. Worse yet, if we continue to ask our feeble elderly parents for hand-outs, we will be condemned as losers. Likewise, the Buddha looks after us when we are not wise. But once we have learned the Buddha's teachings, we can attain Enlightenment by faithfully following them. Would the Buddha be pleased with us if, instead of focusing on Enlightenment, we continuously plead for worldly blessings like money, good health or high social status? No, he would not. Even if the Buddha were to ask us, "Do you need my help?" we should respond, "That's OK, Buddha, I can take care of myself." We should be able to go even one step further and say, "Buddha, let us take care of the world. You can just sit back and relax." We call such a person a bodhisattva[16].

You should aspire to become a bodhisattva instead

---

16. One on the path of Enlightenment working to relieve the suffering of all beings and help them attain Enlightenment.

of a person always asking for assistance from others. If you are ready to aid others, you will always be a helpful person, but if you expect to be helped by others, you will spend your whole life receiving help. Why do you assume that you are going to Hell and hope to be saved by Bodhisattva Ksitigarbha[17]? If you set your mind on becoming someone like Bodhisattva Ksitigarbha yourself, you won't go to Hell. Even if you do, it won't be a problem since you would be doing your job of saving sentient beings from Hell. Why would you want to be like someone whose business has failed and needs to be saved by others? If you always want to receive help, you will be a needy person all your life. Instead, why not focus on becoming a successful person who can reach out to others in need. You can become a helpful person if

17. The bodhisattva who is willing to go to Hell himself so that he can save all suffering beings.

you set your mind to it.

One day, a woman asked me a question that goes like this. She told me that since she got married to her husband, an eldest son in his family, she had had to take care of all her husband's brothers and sisters until they got married. She went on to say that she was at the end of her rope because, despite all she had done for them, they continued to ask for financial help. Lamenting her situation, she asked me if she had done something wrong in her past life to deserve such a burden. After listening to her predicament, I asked her, "Would you rather be someone who never helps others and to whom no one ever comes for help?" She said that was what she wanted, so I told her, "If that's what you want, just wait a while. You will lose everything you possess." In disbelief, she asked me, "Why am I going to lose everything?" My response was, "If you are broke, no one will come to you asking for help."

Not wanting people coming to you for help is just like praying, "Buddha, please make me poor." Don' t be so foolish. You should always be happy when someone asks you for help. You should be thankful that you have a little bit more than others so that you are able to share and help them in some way.

A person who acts this way is called a bodhisattva. When we aspire to be a bodhisattva, we become generous, compassionate and blessed with healthy mind and body. The reason we cannot become bodhisattvas is that we actually choose to remain sentient beings. We are always pleading, "Please, help me with this, and help me with that." What are we really saying? We are actually saying, "Please, let me forever be a sentient being." That' s why we cannot get even a single step closer to Enlightenment even though we may have been practicing Buddhism for 30 years.

From now on, let' s aspire to become a bodhisattva

and follow the footsteps of the Buddha. Help others whenever you can, and try to understand others instead of wanting to be understood by them. Please become someone who is always trying to benefit the world in some way. As long as you live that way, you'll be all right, no matter what happens.

16

When Unsure About How to Meditate And Do Prostrations

- Recognizing what you are doing wrong and trying again

It's easy to see the flaws in others
But hard to see one's own.
One sifts out the flaws in others like chaff
But hides one's own,
Like a gambler concealing an unfavorable hand.

I experience so many emotional afflictions when I pray and meditate. One thought after another from the past, present and future races through my mind. How should I meditate and do prostrations?

When you sit down to meditate, you would think that your body and mind would relax. But in reality, you are flooded with thoughts about the past and the present as well as plans or fantasies about the future. These are emotional afflictions. Since they arise incessantly, they won't disappear even if you do prostrations or shake your head in an attempt to get rid of them.

Each type of meditation has a particular objective. When we do breathing meditation, our objective is to observe our breath as we inhale and exhale. We need to be aware that we are breathing in when we inhale and breathing out when we exhale. We should also become aware of whether our breathing is deep or shallow. This is called being awake to our breathing, which means our minds are totally focused on it. Likewise, if we meditate on a koan[18], the aim is to concentrate only on the koan. In short, we have to

---

18. A riddle that has no logical solution, which practitioners focus on while meditating.

focus all our mental energy on the objective of our meditation. It means being awake to what we are doing. However, this is not as easy as it sounds because we face so many obstacles when we try to concentrate.

The first obstacle is external hindrances. Right when we try to concentrate, we get distracted and lose our focus because we hear someone rummaging through a bag, a cell phone ringing or someone next to us talking. We are easily sidetracked by external hindrances such as what we experience through our senses of sight, sound, smell, taste and touch. But we shouldn't let these things disturb us. We must concentrate totally on our minds no matter what we see, hear or feel. Admittedly, it's not an easy thing to do. For example, the more we try to tune out car noises, the more we tend to hear them. Therefore, we need to stop blaming the external factors and wishing that they would go away. Instead we should focus on our breathing all the more. Then, even though we can still hear the car noises, they will not interfere with our meditation.

The second obstacle is the physical sensations that arise in our bodies. When we sit cross-legged for a long time, our legs begin to ache and eventually become numb, so we are distracted by these uncomfortable sensations. As a result, we lose our concentration as we begin to debate in our heads whether or not we should stretch out our legs. We may also feel an itch on our faces, as if a bug were trying to bite us, so we get the urge to touch our faces. Nonetheless, we should just let everything be when we are meditating, even when our legs go numb, our faces itch, our backs hurt, or whatever other sensation may arise in our bodies. We should focus only on our breathing.

The third obstacle is emotional afflictions. Past memories and future concerns arise endlessly in our minds. Also, an incident that happened a moment ago lingers in our head and distracts us. After being completely drawn to the incident for a while, we suddenly come to our senses and realize that our minds have wandered as if we were dreaming. Being distracted, we lose track of time and have no idea when it was that we stopped observing our breath.

The sensations in our bodies, various sounds and shapes in the outside world and the constant flow of thoughts in our minds neither disappear nor stop arising simply because we want them to. We hear sounds because we are alive. We have sensations because we have a body. And a constant stream of thoughts runs through our minds whenever we close our eyes because our accumulated experiences have been etched into our consciousness. All of these things arise for a reason, and it is no use to want these sensations and thoughts to stop occurring. Therefore, we should refrain from thinking about them altogether. In other words, we will only make ourselves miserable by trying to stop these things from arising when we don't have the ability to do so. It is analogous to a room becoming dustier the more we dust it.

Whether you hear sounds, feel sensations arising in your body or have thoughts running through your head, you should not get distracted. Despite your efforts, you will surely keep losing track of your breathing. However, distracting thoughts won't get in the way if you persistently bring your focus back to your breathing. Even if you hear noises outside, it won't distract you from observing your breathing. The same applies to physical pain. You will be aware of the pain but will still be able to maintain your concentration. Slowly but surely, before you know it, your mind will become more calm and clear.

You should accept the fact that it's natural for emotional afflictions to arise in your mind. Doubting yourself with thoughts such as, "I shouldn't have emotional afflictions, so why do I have them?" or "Why does my mind race every time I sit down?" is only adding more emotional afflictions on top of the ones you already have. No matter what deceptive thoughts arise, just let them pass by like flowing water and remain focused on the objective of your practice. As you repeat this process, distracting thoughts will naturally fade away on their own.

Likewise, it's good to have a goal when doing prostrations, and what you establish as a goal is important. For example, if your objective is to become humble, you will remind yourself to be humble with each prostration. This doesn't mean that you focus only on the words, "I will become humble." Rather, it means that you reflect upon your actions of the previous day to assess how humble you have been. After contemplation, you may realize, "I wasn't humble yesterday. I promised myself that I would be,

but I ended up acting arrogant and stubborn again."
When you become aware that you failed to keep the
goal you set for yourself, you are more inclined to
repent. If you don't set a goal, you won't know
when you have done something wrong. If you have a
specific objective in place, however, you will know
when you've failed to live up to it, and you will feel
compelled to repent deeply.

Vowing to never forget the goal of your prayer is
referred to as "high aspiration" in the Buddhist tradition. Realizing, "Oh, I forgot about my goal again, but
I won't forget next time," or "I fell down again, but I
will just get back up." exemplify the spirit of high
aspiration. With this awareness, we repent and try to
do better next time. You should do prostrations with
such a mindset. When we're overconfident and think
we're better than others, our postures change. We
hold our heads up high, throw our shoulders back
and straighten our backs. On the other hand, when

we realize we have done something wrong, we willingly lower our heads, bend our backs, kneel down and touch the ground with our foreheads. Interestingly enough, our emotional afflictions diminish little by little when we do prostrations because it is an act that represents humbling ourselves.

However, since most people do prostrations without a set goal, their minds race with random thoughts. In fact, they are doing prostrations only mechanically with doubts such as, "What am I doing prostrations for? Will anything change because I am doing this? I may need to repent, but does it mean that the other person didn't do anything wrong?" Doing prostrations in this manner may be good physical exercise, but it won't bring lasting changes to your life. If you want your life to change, you need to attain mindfulness by doing repentance prayer based on an objective. Specifically, you need to catch yourself when your behavior is not aligned with your goal and realize, "Oh, I made a mistake. I'll try again," or "I messed up. I'll try once more."

If you continue to practice this way, you will be motivated to do better even when you make the same mistake again. If you fail 100 times, you simply try again for the 101st time. When you contemplate your objective while doing prostrations, your desire to improve gets stronger the more you fail, and you will obtain a sudden awareness. You will be able to catch yourself at the very moment you feel unwilling to be humble. The moment you want to say "No," you become aware and immediately change the answer in your mind to "Yes." Then, you will notice that your heart feels heavy right when you say "No," but you feel relieved the instant you change your mind and say "Yes." At that moment, you experience, "Ah. This is how the mind works."

After having experienced success, you may feel that you will be able to maintain the awareness of your mind and change yourself, but you are likely to fail the next time you try. Fortunately, however, the probability of success will increase with time. For example, if you initially succeed after 100 attempts, you will need only 50 tries the next time. Later on, you may need only 10 tries, five tries, and so on. As such, change comes gradually. At first, you falter most of the time. But after a while, you will have many successes and fail only occasionally, which is an indication that you have progressed a great deal. The change turns a stubborn and difficult person into an accommodating one. You will become considerate and flexible. You will benefit the most by these changes in yourself, but others will benefit and enjoy them too.

There is an old Korean saying that goes, "People won't change unless they're close to death," which illustrates how difficult it is for a person to actually change. However, practice allows us to reform ourselves even when we are not close to death. Changing can be compared to being reborn. Practice can completely transforms our personalities and our fates.

17

When You Feel Too Lazy to Pray

- Great determination that enables you to change your karma

He who
Fails to put forth effort when he should
Wastes youth and good health with laziness
Is filled with delusions and weak resolve
One such as this
Cannot attain the wisdom of Enlightenment.

Even though I know I should practice, I always give in to what my body wants to do. I regret being lazy and idle day after day, but I don't do anything about it. I end up missing my morning prayer every day. I would like to know why I am so lazy.

People usually say, "I want to get up, but my body

won't listen to me." They label this a physical temptation and believe that the body is an obstacle to practice, but that's not true.

According to the Heart Sutra "Form is emptiness," and because the body is form, it is also empty. Emptiness is neither good nor bad, neither sacred nor profane and neither pure nor impure. There is nothing wrong with the body.

The mind is the real problem. That is, the mind is guided by one's karma. Let's say you go to bed intending to get up at 5 a.m. to pray. But when the alarm goes off, you make excuses saying that even though you tell yourself, "I've got to get up... I've got to get up..." your body just doesn't listen to you. However, you fail to see the true nature of things. You do not perceive things as they are. Saying, "I've got to get up..." really means that you don't want to get up. You are actually saying, "I don't want to get up, I don't want to, I don't want to..." In such a case, you are less likely to get up. As a result, you end up not getting up. You can simply continue to sleep if you don't want to get up. It's just fine if you can't practice because you don't want to get up early in the morning. I bet 99 percent of the world's population does not practice. Nobody worries about whether or not you practice, and your life will go on as usual without it. So there is no need to practice if you don't want to.

This not only applies to praying, but to other situations as well. You'll be late for work if you get up late. You can show up late for work, but there are consequences if you do. You should just accept them willingly. If you are fired as a result, just pack up your things and leave. Why would anybody want to work with an employee who is always tardy due to over-sleeping? As you can see, oversleeping and being late to work will bring you repercussions of being reprimanded, denounced or fired. Similarly, if you are tempted to steal something you see on the street, you can do so, but there will be a consequence for your action. They can include humiliation, condemnation or even some jail time. Therefore, should you decide to steal, simply accept the outcome, be it condemnation or a prison sentence. If someone says, "You were sent to jail? You poor thing..." your response should be "Of course I should be in jail for stealing. Even I would send a thief like me to jail." Willingly accepting the negative results of your actions will enable you to live a more peaceful life.

However, the problem is that most people begin to regret their actions when they get reprimanded or lose their jobs. Regretting waking up late, "It's because I overslept. I should have gotten up earlier ...," becomes the source of your suffering. So, the solution is clear. If you don't want to suffer from remorse, just get up even when you don't feel like it. And, you should not eat rat poison if you know what it is no matter how good it looks or how hungry you are. However, people ask, "Can' t I eat just a little bit of it? I am really hungry." You can, but you will die as a consequence. There is no problem if you can say to yourself at the time of your death, "I don' t mind dying because I ate what I wanted to my heart' s content." But if you regret it, thinking, "I should have exercised more self-control and refrained from eating it," then you will feel tormented.

When the consequence of an action is as damaging as it is in this case, you should not let yourself follow the current of your karma. Rather, you must go against it. You should get up at once even though you don' t feel like it. Also, do the things you need to do without procrastinating and just stop taking actions that will bring you negative consequences. You must do so in order to avoid a bigger suffering. In this case, you are not doing it for someone else. You are protecting yourself from a great potential loss.

When it's time for your morning prayer, just get up even though you don't want to. "How can I get up when I don't want to?" you may ask. The answer is you just do it without thinking about it. When the alarm goes off, arise at once before the thought, "I have to get up..." even occurs to you. Even having the thought "I have to get up..." means you are being controlled by your karma. When the alarm rings, spring up instantly. If you do, the thought "I have to get up..." will not occur to you. Such a thought only comes when you don't get up at once.

However, it is very hard for a beginner to practice on his own. If you practice alone, you will find it difficult to go against your karma and you are likely to be lazy. Thus, when you are starting out, if possible, it's best to go to a temple for your morning prayer. In other words, it is easier to practice with others. After doing it for about 100 days, your body will have gotten used to the ritual, and you will find it much easier to do morning prayer on your own at home.

When people begin to practice, they say it's difficult to resist the temptations of their bodies. However, in reality, it is their deeply ingrained habits that they are unable to overcome because people have a natural tendency to keep doing what they have been doing for a long time. Nonetheless, it is not impossible for people to change their habits or go against their karma. It's just very challenging to do so. Why is it so hard? It's mostly because people don't have a genuine intention of changing their habits, so they end up repeating them. For example, you know that you shouldn't nag, but nagging words just slip out of your mouth because of your old habit. No matter how much you want to stop nagging your husband, you just cannot stop. There is a simple way to fix this. Tell your husband, "Please do me a favor and smack me on my back as hard as you can whenever you feel like I'm nagging at you. Then, I

will reward you with $100 each time you smack me."
Try it. If you do, you will be able to break your habit
in no time. It's not that you cannot change your
habits; deep down, you really don't have the desire
to change them. Thus, you continue to live with your
old habits.

No matter how strong your karma is, you can
change it when you have a "great determination."
Karma can only be defeated by "great determination,"
so you need to establish an unshakable "great determination" in your mind. Rather than just deciding to
wake up at 5 a.m. every day to pray, do something
that can reinforce your firm resolve, such as making
yourself pay a $100 fine every time you fail to arise at
5 a.m. If I announce to temple goers that anyone who
attends the morning Dharma service at 5 a.m
tomorrow will receive $1,000, I bet 99 percent of
them will show up. People cannot attain Enlightenment because they don't have this kind of "great

determination." Even though you think, "I'll wake up at 5 a.m. to pray every day," from deep down in your mind your karma creeps up and whispers, "Do I really have to do that? I've lived just fine until now without praying." This is the so-called Devil's temptation described in the sutras. You are enticed by your karma and ask yourself, "Do I really need to pray while on vacation?" and "Does practice have to be so inflexible?" You may think, "It's OK to skip a day of prayer on special occasions like today." As a result, you eventually stop praying.

However, if you adhere to the "great determination" that you will pray no matter what, whether you are on a train or at an airport, there will be no room for temptation to sneak in. A Muslim taxi driver, even with a passenger in the car, will stop driving his taxi at prayer time so he can pray. What's more amazing, the passenger doesn't complain. That's because all devout Muslims do this without exception. Thus, everyone accepts it as a fact of life and becomes accustomed to it. This is a perfect example of a "great determination." If you resolve to do what you set your mind on and do it without fail, no one in the world can get in your way. The people around you will accept and live within the boundary you have set.

For instance, if you resolve to pray at a Buddhist temple every Wednesday, you can tell your family and friends, "Every Wednesday, consider me as someone who doesn' t even exist." Then you go and pray at the temple. To your children you should say, "On Wednesdays, you need to fix yourself something to eat because I won' t be home." In return, you need to be very accommodating to your children at all other times. You should not nag at them or scold them even if they come home late. You should also prepare tasty meals for them. Then, your children will accept your decision and adjust to the change. Even if you work for a company, you can go to the temple after work every Wednesday without exception. Eventually, your friends or colleagues will avoid scheduling a gathering or a party on Wednesdays. If mutual benefit can be obtained within the boundary you have set, other people will accept your decision and live with it.

Unfortunately, most of you lack this "great determination." What do you think is the reason? It's because you don't pay sincere and earnest homage to the Dharma. For example, a smoker's habit of smoking doesn't go away easily. If the smoker stops smoking, his old habit will make him sick and extremely anxious. The biochemical imbalance in his body will force him to smoke again, so the smoker cannot overcome his habit. Having a "great determination" means saying to your karma, "You do what you want; I will do what I have to do." and then following through with your decision. Although your karma will put up a strong fight, it will eventually die out on its own.

You need such an attitude for steadfast practice. If you resolve to practice, you should do it with a "great determination." If you have decided to defer to your husband in order to make your life truly happy, you should not be bothered even if he drinks heavily, wastes money or has an extramarital affair. Those things are trivial compared to the important task of changing your karma. You should support him by saying, "Well done," regardless of what your husband does. Even if he comes home completely drunk, brings home a mistress, or quits his job, you should be able to say, "Well done! Good job!" But people usually reach a point when they feel, "This is the last straw. I cannot tolerate it anymore," so they end up failing to change their karma.

To attain Enlightenment, you should be able to regard worldly concerns as insignificant. Only then will your practice become easier and will there be no room for temptations along the way. Considering how hard it is to change one's karma, it is difficult for most of you to attain Enlightenment unless you have an intense desire and motivation for practice. Only when you persevere without letting go of your "great determination" will you be able to extinguish your karma and attain Enlightenment.

18

When You Cannot Do Prostrations Because You Are Physically Unable

- Prostrating, a way of expressing a humble mind

If one gives up a lesser happiness
One acquires the greatest happiness.
A wise person
Renounces the lesser happiness
And awaits the outcome of the greatest happiness, Enlightenment.

Some people have told me that they feel bad about not being able to do prostrations because of their ill health. If doing prostrations numerous times was equivalent to making good progress in practice, healthy people would be the best practitioners. The reason we do prostrations is far more important than the number of prostrations we do.

Prostration is a way of expressing one's humble mind while repenting, "I was wrong, and I was ignorant." Even if you cannot do prostrations because you are physically unable, humbling your mind can be considered the same as doing prostrations. How much you humble your mind is more important than the number of prostrations you do. Then, some may ask, "Does that mean I don't need to do prostrations if I can maintain a humble state of mind?" Theoretically, yes. However, the question can be compared to someone saying arrogantly, "Isn't it enough that I am aware I did something wrong? Do I really need to apologize verbally in person?"

If you are not well enough to do prostrations, you don't have to. However, if you are perfectly healthy, saying, "Do I really have to do prostrations? I am repenting deeply..." really means you actually believe, "Do I really need to crouch over and sweat from doing prostrations? I don' t think I did anything wrong..."

You need to do 108 prostrations daily, and do 300, 500, 1,000, even 3,000 prostrations if necessary. The body follows the mind, and the mind follows the body. At first you might be reluctant to do prostrations, but if you continue doing them, your mind will eventually become humble. Also, the body will naturally assume a humble posture when your mind repents. Therefore, although you do not need to obsess over the number of prostrations, it is best to do them slowly and consistently even when you are not feeling your best.

19

Morning Prayer, Evening Prayer
- Overcoming the reluctance to pray

It is a pleasure to have a friend when you need one.
The biggest pleasure is sharing your joy with others.
If you have done many good deeds,
You will be happy at the end of your life.
What is even more pleasing is leaving behind all suffering.

There are some people who find it physically too demanding to do prostrations in the morning. If it's hard to pray in the morning, try praying in the evening, but you need to do it consistently every evening. It is not a good idea to pray at random times of the day, such as during the day today, in the morning tomorrow, and at night the day after tomorrow.

Your desire or reluctance to pray depends on your individual karma, how you have lived your life up to this point. Therefore, if you let your karma dictate your actions, praying won't do you any good. We practice in order to overcome our reluctance to do something. The reason it feels so taxing on your body to pray in the morning is that you are forcing yourself to do it when you don't really want to.

For now, try praying in the evenings as you wish. However, keep in mind that you will often be unable to pray because you are likely to encounter situations that will keep you from doing your prayer. For instance, your family members may come home, you may have a guest over, or you may get home late from work. On the other hand, if you wake up at 5 a.m. to do prostrations, you will most likely not be interrupted. That's why it is better to pray early in the morning.

In conclusion, if you feel better praying in the

evening and are able to do it every day at a set time, by all means, pray in the evening. However, if you keep missing your evening prayer for one reason or another, you should pray early in the morning. Once you decide to pray in the morning, you should not do it reluctantly. That won't help you make progress with your practice. You should wake up at 5 a.m. without any resistance and pray lightheartedly. At first you may feel disinclined to pray, but try to pray with a positive frame of mind. With time you will be able to overcome your reluctance. This is how you can change your karma.

20

Merit of Sutra Copying in Buddhism

- Awakening to the Dharma

From moment to moment,
Correctly observing the arising and disappearing of Feelings,
We will obtain joy and happiness
And gain the wisdom that transcends death.

A person asked me whether one can earn merit from copying the Buddhist sutras. Yes, there is value in sutra copying. However, if you place too much importance on earning merit, Buddhism becomes solely a means of obtaining merit. If you want sutra copying to help you attain Enlightenment, you need to grasp the meaning of the sutra while copying it down. It will be easier for you to understand the content of the sutra when you read it carefully, paying careful attention to the meaning as compared to when you breeze through it. Needless to say, you will obtain a deeper understanding of the meaning if you take time and read the sutra while copying down each word with care.

However, you should not expect that the amount of merit you earn will be higher when you copy a Buddhist sutra compared to when you just read it. The same applies to when you copy the sutra 10 times compared to copying it only once. Although you may feel like you are earning more merits, you are not.

Even reading books on general topics can help you lead a better life, so imagine how much more beneficial reading the Buddhist sutra must be. There is merit in reading the sutra even once like a novel. Naturally, it goes without saying that there is more merit in reading it while writing down each word by hand. However, it is important to keep in mind that grasping the meaning of the Buddha's teachings is the purpose of sutra copying. If you simply believe that you will earn merit by copying the sutra, your focus will not be on understanding the meaning of the Dharma. Then, sutra copying becomes a mere act of seeking merit.

21

Praying for Family Members' Well-Being

-Praying diligently while letting go of the thought that I am right

Do not scorn what you have achieved with your ability
Do not envy what others have achieved
A practitioner who is envious of others
Cannot attain the blissful state of true wisdom.

It is true that when one prays diligently, everything will go well for his family. Praying diligently means praying every single day with a certain aspiration. It's a worthy activity. If you exercise for 30 minutes every morning, it will be beneficial for your health and relieve your stress, which could even improve your family relationships. Undoubtedly, doing 108 prostrations every morning, will be helpful to both you and your family members.

When children see their mother praying every morning at 5 a.m. in front of a burning incense all year round regardless of good or bad things happening in the family, they will feel an enormous sense of security. That is why the children of mothers who prayed diligently in front of a bowl of clean water at dawn every day, a common sight in Korea in the old days, generally grew up to be noteworthy people.

Is this only possible in a Buddhist household? No. For example, if a Christian mother prays every morning for an hour, her children will also grow up to be commendable adults. Without strong faith and persistence, it is impossible to pray regularly every morning. In other words, parents' diligence and perseverance have a positive influence on their children. Thus, the saying "When you pray diligently, things will go well for your family" is in fact a true statement. However, this is different from the saying "When I pray for the well-being of my family members, nothing bad will happen to them."

You may believe your prayer can make your husband succeed in his job or help your child get into a good college. However, that's not how prayer works. If someone asks me, "Now that I have started praying, how should I go about it?" I always answer that the prayer should be the practice of letting go of the thought, "I am right." Regardless of whom you pray for – your children, your husband, or your parents – your prayer should be about understanding them from their points of view. There is great merit in the prayer that tries to understand others by reflecting, "That person only acted that way based on his point of view, but I objected to it because I assessed the situation only from my own perspective."

III. One Hour of Happiness

22

Repentance Prayer for Jungto Practitioners

(Generally speaking, there are no specific rules about what rituals should be included in your prayer or about the order in which they should be performed. The following is the manual of Repentance Prayer for Jungto Practitioners. You can set aside a time and a place, including your own home, for your daily prayer.)

Taking Refuge in the Three Jewels

Do prostration as you recite each of the three vows for the Three Jewels.

1. I take refuge in the Buddha.

I pay homage and reverence to the Buddha.

(Do one prostration)

2. I am delighted to learn the Dharma.

   I vow to practice diligently with the knowledge that everything is the result of my own deeds.

(Do one prostration)

3. I am proud to be a disciple of the Buddha.

I vow to become a bodhisattva, liberating all beings from suffering.

(Do one prostration)

Words for Practice

(Kneel down and read aloud the prayer manual. It is important to reinforce the meaning of the prayer by reading it aloud. Even if the objective of your prayer is good, you won't be able to reach it without clear guidance.)

The root of all suffering and attachments are within us.

Those who don't make the effort to closely reflect upon their own lives mistakenly believe that these suffering and attachments come from the outside. Our attempts to find happiness and freedom by searching various religions, attending many temples and churches, and visiting different teachers are to no avail because the way to peace of mind can never be found outside of our minds.

No matter what kinds of problems we may have, if we reflect deeply, we realize that the root of our afflictions is within us and that the mind itself is empty. With this realization, our suffering naturally disappears. Nevertheless, we still hold onto our opinions and make distinctions of right or wrong, thereby bringing all kinds of suffering onto ourselves.

Once we free ourselves from our attachments, our

suffering will end immediately.

Repentance

When we look outwardly, our anger, frustration, hate and resentment often seem to be caused by others. However, upon introspection, we realize that we are caught up in the notion, "I am right," and that the true cause of suffering actually comes from ourselves. When we realize that nothing is inherently right or wrong in the Dharma and let go of the thought, "I am right," all our suffering and karmic hindrances will disappear.

(Do a half prostration)

108 Prostrations

(Keeping the meaning of repentance and your prayer objective in mind, perform each prostration while reflecting upon and repenting your past actions.)

Meditation (10 minutes)

(Meditate for 10 minutes or more. Assume a meditation posture with your back straight and focus your mind on the tip of your nose. Observe your breathing in and out without being distracted by anything in your surroundings. The purpose of the meditation is to discard your delusions.)

Reading the Sutra

(Read aloud the passage of the Sutra assigned for each day. The purpose of reading the sutra is to shed ignorance and gain wisdom.)

The Vows of the Jungto Practitioners

(Read aloud The Vows of the Jungto Practitioners. The

content explains the high aspiration of Jungto practitioners who have committed themselves to pray for 1,000 days continuously. Remind yourself every day about the values you want to live by and the aspirations you want to achieve.)

Our modern civilization is facing a serious crises. People are losing their humanity, communities are disintegrating, and the natural environment is being destroyed. We look to the teachings of the Buddha to find solutions to these problems.

We base our perspective of world on the Law of Interdependence.

As this exists, that exists, and if this ceases to exist that will also cease to exist. This is the state of things as they are. Since everything is interdependent, your death signifies my death, and your survival means my survival. Also, your unhappiness turns into my unhappiness, and your happiness leads to my happiness. Based on this dependent origination, we pursue the path we can live together in happiness. Just as a variety of flowers makes up a garden and the diversity of people creates harmony and balance, we wish to form a new civilization in which love overcomes jealousy and envy, cooperation triumphs over confrontation and competition, and peace prevails over conflict and war.

We take the Buddha and bodhisattvas as the models for our own lives.

Following the footsteps of the Buddha, who lived an austere life with only one set of robes and one food bowl, we assume the mindset of a practitioner by eating more mindfully and living more frugally and diligently, unhindered by anything in the world. Furthermore, we look to the Compassionate Bodhisattva Avalokite-shvara[19] who embraces the pain of all beings, and the Great Vows Bodhisattva Kshiti-garbba[20], who even goes to Hell to save all beings, as our role models. Finally, we vow to be Mahayana Bodhi-sattvas[21], who saves all sentient beings from suffering.

We uphold the principles of non-ego, non-possession and non-obstinacy in our practice.

With the aim of creating Jungto[22], we vow to sur-render our egos, our possessions and our obstinacy to become bodhisattvas who solely cater to the needs of sentient beings. By changing our mindset we hope to

19. The bodhisattva of infinite compassion and mercy.

20. The bodhisattva who is willing to go to Hell himself so that he can save all suffering beings.

21. They are Enlightened beings who work for the Enlightenment of all beings, not just for themselves.

become free of attachments and suffering. Furthermore, we vow to overcome the crisis impending on our civilization by creating Jungto, a world in which individuals are happy, communities are peaceful and the natural environment is preserved.

Ten Guidelines along the Path (Bowang Sammaeron)

(Read aloud these 10 guidelines of Bowang Sammaeron)

1. Consider illness as your medicine.

Do not wish for perfect health. Perfect health makes it easy for you to be greedy. Thus, the Buddha said, "Consider illness as your medicine."

---

22. Pure land or "Land of Bliss" is a paradise where Amitabha Buddha, whose hope is to bring all being into it, is believed to reside.

2. Accept your worries and hardships as part of life.

Do not wish for a life free from hardship. Such a life leads only to arrogance and self-pampering. Thus, the Buddha said, "Accept your worries and hardships as part of life."

3. Attain Nirvana amidst the hindrances.

Do not wish to be free of hindrances in your practice. Without hindrances, it will be hard to advance in your practice. Thus, the Buddha said, "Attain Nirvana amidst the hindrances."

4. Treat temptation as a friend who helps you in your practice.

Do not hope to be free from temptation in your practice. Without temptations, your resolve cannot become strong. Thus, the Buddha said, "Treat temptation as a friend who helps you in your practice."

5. Persevere through long periods of time to accomplish your goals.

Do not wish for things to work out easily. When things work out easily, one becomes rash. Thus, the Buddha said, "Persevere through long periods of time to accomplish your goals."

6. Preserve your friendship with pure motives.

Do not wish to benefit from your friendships. Seeking to benefit from your friends will damage the relationship. Thus, the Buddha said, "Preserve your friendship with pure motives."

7. Surround yourself with people who have opinions that are different from yours.

Do not expect others to follow your wishes. If they do, you will become arrogant. Thus, the Buddha said, "Surround yourself with people with different opinions from yours for your practice."

8. Discard the expectation of reward.

Do not expect merits for your good deeds. If you do, you will work only for your self-interest. Thus, the Buddha said, "Discard the expectation of rewards as you would throw away old shoes."

9. Accumulate wealth through modest gains.

Do not expect more than you deserve. Undeserved profit only leads to foolishness. Thus, the Buddha said, "Accumulate wealth through modest gains."

10. Regard unjust treatment as the door to entering spiritual practice.

Refrain from defending your position when feeling unjustly treated. Defending your position will only make the other person become more resentful. So the Buddha said, "Regard unjust treatment as the door to entering spiritual practice."

You will find the solution in the very obstacle you face. Efforts to evade difficulties only lead to more problems. Thus, the Buddha found the path to Enlightenment amidst the obstacles. If people seeking the Truth cannot endure life's difficulties, they cannot surmount the hurdles in their practice and attain the treasures of the Dharma. Therefore, overcoming adversities leads us to the path toward Enlightenment.

The Four Great Vows

(Finally, we recite the Four Great Vows.)

1. I vow to create Jungto, the land of Bliss where no sentient beings suffer. (Do a half prostration)

2. I vow to end all suffering and emotional afflictions through practice. (Do a half prostration)

3. I vow to learn all of the Buddha's teachings. (Do a half prostration)

4. I vow to attain Buddhahood along with all sentient beings. (Do a half prostration)

Practice Journal

(After completing your prayer, record your thoughts daily in the practice journal. You may write down any thoughts that occurred or emotions experienced during prayer. For example, "I didn't feel like praying" or "I repent that I got angry yesterday." By doing so, you become aware of the changes taking place within you.)

Almsgiving and Good Deeds

(Practice generosity by donating more than one dollar a day with the aim of overcoming greed. Also, do at least one good deed daily or do volunteer work for good causes. This sums up the explanation of Repentance Prayer for Jungto Practitioners.)

23

Taking Refuge in the Three Jewels

I hold the utmost admiration and respect for the Buddha.

I take refuge in the Buddha in the sincerest way.

I am delighted to have found the Dharma.

I will practice diligently because I know everything that happens to me is the result of my own deeds.

I am proud to be a disciple of the Buddha.

I vow to become a bodhisattva, liberating all sentient beings in the world from suffering.

The Purpose of Life

"Taking Refuge in the Three Jewels" signifies that we rely on the Three Jewels for guidance in our practice. The Three Jewels are the most important three treasures to Buddhists: the Buddha, the Dharma, and the Sangha[23]. Why do Buddhists chant "Taking Refuge in the Three Jewels" at the beginning of a Buddhist ceremony or prayer? The reason is to make clear that the purpose of our life is to attain Enlightenment just as the Buddha attained true freedom and Nirvana. Being Enlightened means becoming a person free from suffering and all constraints in life. Regardless of how many noble accomplishments you have in life, if you are unhappy, they are merely the activities of a sentient being. The ultimate goal of practice is to be liberated and to be free of suffering. You should never lose sight of this whether you are working or practicing.

---

23. Buddhist monastic order, traditionally composed of four groups: monks, nuns, laymen, and laywomen.

A Free Person Without Suffering

What kind of people are liberated and without suffering? They are the ones who are in charge of their own destinies. Such people do not resent or blame others. Even when they struggle and fail to achieve their goals, they gather themselves up and begin anew each time. Only children make a big fuss and ask others to help them up when they fall down. Such a childlike mind is unenlightened, which in turn is the mind of a sentient being.

If you want to become a Buddha, you must take responsibility for your life. There may be times when you want to say, "This is not my fault!" But there shouldn't be any exceptions in practice. That is, if you make any exceptions to the premise that all your suffering comes from your mind, your practice will go astray.

For example, when someone who has borrowed

money from you does not pay it back, as a practitioner, you should not blame the borrower. Instead, you should reflect upon your own actions, realizing, "I was not wise to lend him money." Blaming others and resenting them is inconsistent with the principle of Buddhist practice. When you resent others, you become unhappy and run the risk of losing your money as well as ruining the relationship you had with the borrower. If you think to yourself, "It was foolish of me to lend him money with the idea of getting it back when I should have just given it to him in the first place," you will be able to save your relationship because you will not resent the borrower even if he doesn't pay you back. If you don't ruin the relationship, there is a possibility that he may pay you back someday. However, even if you never get the money back, you can tell yourself lightheartedly, "Maybe I owed him money in my past life."

Practitioners should go one step further and not

even consider this monetary loss as a sacrifice. In the secular world, people who sacrifice themselves fighting for righteous causes are called martyrs. But practitioner is merely born, practices diligently for the sake of practicing, and then passes away. One may momentarily become possessed by the thought that he is right and harbor resentment; however, this resentment should not last long. A practitioner should realize right away, "I have strayed from the path of practice," and set himself back onto the right path. Someone who dwells on hatred and resentment cannot be considered to be a true practitioner. As a practitioner, you must be able to catch yourself blaming others and quickly change your perspective.

That is the way to honor the teachings of the Buddha and become a disciple of the Buddha. This is also called "Taking Refuge in the Three Jewels."

Being the Master of My Life

When you take refuge in the Three Jewels, you become the master of your destiny as well as of the entire universe. There is no one in the world, other than yourself, who will take responsibility for your life. No matter what happens — even if your spouse passes away, has an affair or wants a divorce — if you resent or hate your spouse, you are not the master of your life. If you hate a person, your life becomes dependent on the actions of that person. If your spouse unexpectedly asks for a divorce unexpectedly, you should be able to say, "Yes, I' ve had a wonderful time with you. Thank you." When you reach the level of practice in which you have no feelings of animosity toward your spouse, you can truly become the master of your life.

However, people do not have the wisdom of being the owner of their own lives, so they let others control their lives. If you let your wife, husband, parents or children have the steering wheel of your car, so to speak, you are letting others drive you in any direction they please. Your car will not go where you intended it to go. As a result, you may spend your life saying, "I am miserable because of this or that person," or "I am so happy because of this or that person." That' s why you wallow in agony when your spouse has an affair, your parents pass away, your children cause trouble, your company fails or you have a terminal illness. If you fall into despair because your business has gone bankrupt, you are letting your business be the master of your life.

Even if you cannot be mindful at all times, whenever external circumstances in your life affect you negatively, you must remind yourself "I only lose when I blame others, and that' s not the way to be in control of my own life," and try to have a clear perspective. If you fall into delusion and your teacher tells you, "Wake up! You are a practitioner!" you should let go of your own thoughts and quickly regain the perspective of a practitioner. Even when no one else in the world can persuade you, your teacher should be able to prompt you to see everything with clarity. Someone becomes your teacher, not because of his greatness but because you have decided to honor and respect him as your teacher.

Vowing to Take Refuge in the Three Jewels

Attaining Enlightenment is simple. From now on, regard your husband, wife or parents as your teacher, and defer to them without question, saying, "Yes," to whatever they say or demand. At first, you will find this extremely difficult. Every time you fail, you must reflect and think to yourself, "Ah, I was trapped in my own perception again," and realize how much you tend to insist on your ways. If you are vigilant of your mind, you can attain Enlightenment within three days; otherwise, you may not become Enlightened even in 30 years. If you are not aware of how much you are trapped in your own incorrect perception, it is absolutely of no use even if you chant all day, sit still in meditation for hours and hours like a stone Buddha, do 3,000 prostrations every day, or read the Tripikata Koreana[24]. Your teacher should be the standard by which you measure yourself in your efforts to let go of your ego. If you don't practice in adherence to this principle, you will not make any progress.

When you vow to take refuge in the Three Jewels, you should first realize the meaning of "taking refuge in the Three Jewels" and say, "I admire and respect the Buddha and I take refuge in the Buddha with

---

24. The complete collection of eighty thousand Buddhist sutras, laws and treaties. It is the only remaining complete collection of Buddhist scriptures in the world today, which has been housed for over 700 years in Haein-Sa Temple in South Korea.

sincerest regard." Secondly, because you are lucky enough to have found the Dharma and are on the path to Enlightenment, you should say, "I will practice diligently because I know everything that happens to me is the result of my own deeds." Thirdly, vow to practice the Dharma by proclaiming, "I am proud to be a disciple of the Buddha. I will become a bodhisattva, liberating all sentient beings in the world from suffering."

Since Buddhists always keep these three grand aspirations in mind, they can remain calm and peaceful like the Buddha, regardless of what situation or place they are in. Knowing the correct meaning of the Three Jewels will enable you to be the master of your life.

24

Words for Practice

Upon careful observation, you can see that all suffering and
constraints come from one's mind.
Unwise people, however, are under the delusion that these problems
come from the outside.
Consequently, they seek happiness and freedom in various religions,
temples and people.
Their efforts are in vain because the way to peace of mind can never
be found outside one's mind.

Complete Happiness, Complete Freedom

Emotional pain and constraint together are called suffering. In Buddhism, being free from suffering is called Nirvana, and living without constraints is called liberation. In lay terms, the state in which all suffering is removed is called happiness, and the state in which one is relieved of constraints is called freedom. Therefore, we always speak of freedom and happiness in the same vein. In other words, complete happiness is Nirvana and complete freedom is liberation.

Who is Responsible for All the Suffering and Constraints?

All suffering and constraints originate from one's mind. However, unwise people are under the wrong impression that these are caused by external factors. When asked why they are in anguish, people, without exception, answer that they are suffering because of that person or because of that thing. This means they believe the cause of their suffering comes from their surroundings. When people say, "It is because of that person or that thing," it means that they wish they could control someone or something the way they want. They believe their suffering would disappear if only they could have everything they want. However, since they cannot, they turn to religion in search of a divine entity to solve their problems. People search for the faith that will best meet their needs by comparing various religions. When desperate, this is a natural course of action. People try going to different churches or temples just as they try different kinds of remedies when they are ill.

All in One's Mind

Despite their sincere efforts, people can never find the solution to their problems when they look for the cause of their suffering outside of themselves. This is because the way to peace of mind can never be found outside one's mind. Since the cause of the suffering is not in the external environment, people cannot reach Nirvana by searching for it outside of themselves.

No matter when or where it occurs and how difficult and dire the problem may be, the cause of any suffering resides in our minds. Therefore, if we reflect deeply, we can find out the true nature of the problem. Upon close inspection, we come to realize that the root of the suffering is inside our foolish minds. However, the foolish mind does not exist in reality. If we realize that the true nature of our mind is "emptiness," meaning having no real entity, our sufferings will effortlessly disappear.

Nonetheless, people are caught up in their own thoughts or the "form" that something is right or wrong, thereby creating all kinds of suffering for themselves. Being attached to one's own thoughts means a person has turned his view into an objective truth. According to the Heart Sutra, this is called "distorted view." When people are attached to their own thoughts, they are unable to perceive anything other than, "You did a good job," or "You are right." They can only see and hear comments that further reinforce their views. Therefore, when you suggest they practice, they become irritated, responding abrasively, "What practice? If you like it that much, why don't you practice?" This is because they have already objectified their own thoughts into absolute truths.

It Looks Red to Me

No matter how strong a person's opinion may be, if he is aware that it is his subjective thought, he will eventually be able to open his eyes to the objective truth. For example, if a person with red lenses looks at a wall and says, "It looks red to me," he is speaking from his subjective standpoint. Since he is aware of this, when he hears someone say, "It looks blue to me," he will acknowledge, "It looks red to me, but I guess it looks blue to that person." Therefore, he feels no need to argue with the other person.

However, a person who believes his perception is objective will insist, "The wall is red," rather than saying, " It looks red to me." When he hears someone say, "That wall is blue," he will retort, " Is something wrong with your eyes? How can that wall look blue?" If that person answers, "No, You shouldn't think you are always right." He may momentarily pretend to yield, "Yes, I guess you are right." However, as soon as he turns his back, he will say to himself, " But, I am still right."

Ask any stubborn person if he considers himself to be stubborn. None of them will admit it. If a person asks, "Am I stubborn?" he is actually not that stubborn. However, if a person says, "I am not stubborn at all." he is, in fact, as stubborn as a mule. An extremely obstinate person has no clue he's so intractable; if he knew, he wouldn't continue to be that hardheaded.

Ask any drunken person if he's drunk. Chances are you won't be able to find a single drunken person who will admit he is inebriated. He will probably respond, "Who says I'm drunk? I'm completely sober!" with his speech slurred and body swaying. On the other hand, a person who asks, "Am I a little drunk?" is actually not that intoxicated.

Generally speaking, women tend to be more willful than men. Men raise their voices but are usually not very stubborn. On the other hand, if a woman is strongly asserting her opinion and a man responds by shouting at her, she will pretend to acquiesce. However, she will think to herself, "What a crazy guy," and disregard him. She will say to herself, "You don't know anything, yet you are so arrogant. You are not even worth talking to," and she will remain completely aloof and silent. Based on her outward reaction, the man might believe the woman has conceded, but that's far from the truth. As a matter of fact, she will shut him out of her life, concluding, "You are not worth my time, and you don't deserve to be treated with respect." This is a good example of being stubborn like a mule.

Also, when it comes to being stubborn, a nice person is more unyielding than a mean person. I'm not saying being kind is a bad thing. People who misbehave usually to know that they are somewhat bad, but nice people always think, "I'm right," so it's difficult for them to let go of their own opinions. Since cordial people are often praised by others, they cannot imagine being wrong in any way. It is hard to convince such people to yield to other people's opinions because they tend to be self-righteous.

Enclosed by One's Own Thoughts

As mentioned earlier, people are caught up in their own thoughts or the "form" that something is right or wrong, thereby creating all sorts of suffering for themselves. Rather than thinking, "To me, it looks…" they objectify their own thoughts and make judgments about what is right or wrong. If they can discard their tendency to make such distinctions, all of their suffering and constraints will vanish.

Our suffering and constraints are webs we have created for ourselves. The way to untangle ourselves from them is to recognize that the cause of the problem is not outside but in our minds. We also need to understand that these webs do not actually exist in reality. With this knowledge, practitioners should devote themselves to practice so they can attain ultimate happiness and freedom.

25
Words for Repentance

All our feelings of anger, irritation, hatred and resentment,
When looking outwardly, may seem to be caused by
the wrongdoings of others.
However, upon introspection, we see that they stem from
the thought, "I am right."
When we realize that, in Truth, there is no absolute right or wrong,
Let go of the thought, "I am right."
Then, all of suffering will disappear,
and all kinds of karma will be dissolved.

The Right Path of Practice

We seek to achieve Nirvana by taking refuge in the
Three Jewels – the Buddha, the Dharma, and the
Sangha – and by practicing the Three Vehicles toward
Enlightenment moral precept (Gye), meditation (Jeong),

and wisdom (Hye). However, in order to observe the precepts among the Three Vehicles toward Enlightenment, we have to first agree to the moral values. In regards to the precept of "refrain from taking life," it is hard to observe the precept if we view it negatively, "How can we possibly live without taking life?" We have to fully embrace the value and make a pledge, "I should absolutely refrain from killing even the smallest living thing." Even if we understand and fully agree with the precept, we tend to break it because of the way we have lived our lives until now – our lifestyle, our ways of thinking and our habits. Also, in our daily life, there are times when we encounter situations in which we cannot help but break the precept. This is the point at which the practice of repentance can begin.

We should not break the precept in the first place, but when we do, we should become aware of what we have done. With the awareness, we should repent and resolve to adhere to the precept the next time. When faced with external obstacles, we tend to become defensive and choose selfish actions. Consumed with the thought of defending and benefitting the "self," we unintentionally harm, harass or deceive others. In such instances, we should become aware that what we are doing is wrong. Therefore, in order to do the practice of repentance, we need to know what the right path is, follow it and recognize when we have deviated from it. In practice, we always need to be mindful of everything we do.

True Repentance

When people are asked to repent, they kneel down to prostrate, saying, "It was my fault." However, this is not repentance. It is actually equivalent to praying, "Buddha, please give me good fortune." They merely go through the motion of doing prostrations because they believe repentance will dissipate future disasters and bring them good fortune. Repentance begins with becoming aware of one's own wrongdoings.

In figuring out of what you did wrong, what would be the criteria for discerning what is right or wrong? The most important criterion is knowing that fundamentally there is no right or wrong. Since there is no right or wrong to begin with, we have to repent our mistake in having judged something to be right or wrong. Generally, when we repent, we tend to think, "You were right, and I was wrong. Therefore, I need to repent." However, this is the repentance of those who make distinction between right or wrong. True repentance is apologizing for having made the mistake of thinking that there is such a thing as right or wrong when in reality all things are merely different. Since there is no right or wrong, there is no reason for us to hate or get angry with others. Unfortunately, we view the world with our subjective perception, mistaking our perception to be the objective view of the world. In other words, we objectify the thoughts that arise from our own karma and incorrectly conclude that there is right or wrong. When we believe other people's ways are wrong, we resent and get angry at them, for which we need to repent.

As such, when we admit, "It was my fault," we should repent for our ignorance rather than for our wrongdoing. It is because our fault lies in hating, cursing and fighting with others, all of which stemmed from our ignorance. If we repent about the action itself rather than our ignorance, we may think, "I repent, since what I did was wrong, and what you did was right." Then, next time, we may demand of others, "You need to repent since you are at fault for doing this." As a result, we end up repenting only at certain times based on our personal discretion.

Generally, people think they are right most of the

time and rarely concede that others can also be right. For example, if they think they are right 100 times, they may admit that others are right only about five times. However, when we begin to practice, we realize, "Other people were right 100 times, while I was right only about five times." If we think this way, we are unable to repent about the five times that we thought we were right. Unfortunately, this is not practice. Practice is unequivocally realizing, "Everything originates from my mind." Therefore, only when we realize "There is no right or wrong" can we truly repent every single time, be it 100 times or even 10,000 times.

Therefore, we must repent if we feel anguish, harbor hatred or get angry. We need to repent for prejudices we have about others and for our ignorance that makes us hate, blame, and shout at them. Finally, only with the full understanding of the principle that there is no right or wrong, can we truly repent.

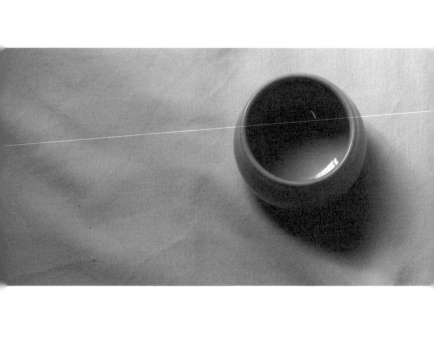

IV. Letting Go

26

Being Awake to the Present and Recognizing Emptiness

Remaining in a peaceful and quiet place,
A practitioner will gain peace of mind,
Experience heavenly joy
And clearly grasp the profound meaning of the truth.

People say they have great suffering, but when they look deeply into it, they realize that suffering doesn't have a real entity. Likewise, you may claim something as yours, but upon further investigation, you realize there is nothing that you can call your own. There are no such things as "good or bad," "virtuous or evil," or "pretty or ugly," in the world. A thing is simply the way it is. This concept is called "emptiness." Once you realize that all things are "empty," the distinctions you used to make disappear. Therefore, there is nothing to agonize over in life.

It is the same with the emotion of fear. Just as people get scared when they encounter a robber in a dream, they become anxious when they are seized by an illusion. Once you experience, with both mind and body, that, "All things are empty, therefore, there is nothing to fear," you will no longer harbor fearful thoughts. However, if you understand this only intellectually, you will become frightened again when you face a certain external condition. This is why it is important to practice "just to be aware" at all times. When you sense that fear is arising in you. You should be mindful, "I am feeling fearful." Do not be frightened or run away. Instead, simply be aware, "I am feeling fearful. I am worried. I am experiencing panic. I am feeling scared," and so on.

Fear does not actually exist. It arises because of an illusion. You may be afraid of snakes, but in reality, the snakes themselves do not elicit fear. They simply look the way they do, but you happen to perceive them with fear. That's why you get scared momentarily when someone taunts you with a toy snake. You react with horror without being conscious of it. Since the association of snakes with fear is deeply ingrained in your unconscious, this particular reaction arises spontaneously when you encounter the external condition, which, in this case, is a snake or toy snake.

The purpose of observing our breathing during meditation is to be aware of the inhales as the air flows in and the exhales as the air flows out through our noses. Everyone knows that when we breathe, the air travels in and out through our noses. However, when we sit in a meditative posture and try to observe our breathing, we find that it is not an easy task. Simply knowing that we breathe and being aware of our breathing are not the same. It is an indication of how distracted we are by our own thoughts. Our minds are not focused on the present. This is largely due to the fact that we have not led our lives with clear mindfulness until now. As a result, during meditation, we may be able to observe our breathing for a very short time but soon become distracted and lose our concentration.

27

Practice Diligently
like the Constant Dripping of Water
That Wears Away the Stone

Severing all worldly ties and having no fear,
With no attachments,
And free of worldly desires,
I call him a practitioner.

When we have a nightmare, we suffer because we believe the dream is real. However, if the nightmare occurs repeatedly two or three times, we eventually realize, even in our dream, that we are only dreaming. Realizing that it is only a dream when we are dreaming is practice. We need to be mindful even while we are dreaming.

Likewise, when the feelings of agony, anger, and hatred surge within us, we have to be aware, "My negative emotions are being stirred up by external conditions." It is important to train our minds to be vigilant of the arising of our emotions. Doing prostrations alone will not improve our mindfulness. In fact, there is no single special method that will do the trick. When a feeling arises, always try to be aware of it right away, realizing, "Oh, I let my feelings overtake me." When you fail to be aware of an emotion arising at the moment, you must continue to practice so you can succeed the next time. In other words, try to be aware of what is going on in your mind at all times.

If you continuously repeat this process, it will become easier for you to be aware of a feeling precisely at the moment it begins to arise in you. Then, you will notice that your feeling naturally recede. Consequently, your behavior will not be controlled by it. Therefore, continuous and rigorous training is needed. This is practice.

When attempting a new skill, we normally try a few times, but when we don't succeed we tend to blame the Buddha, God, our ancestors, or our own fates. However once, we have found the correct path, we need to practice with steadfast diligence. We must repeat the process endlessly even when we fail. Only with such perseverance, can we dissolve our karma and change our habits.

No matter how polluted water gets, it can be purified. Water itself cannot become dirty. Water becomes polluted only when it is mixed with other elements, not because its inherent nature has changed. Just as water can be purified when the impurities are removed, anyone can have a pure mind when greed, anger and ignorance are tamed.

"Practice diligently like the constant dripping of water that makes a hole in the stone." These were the final words of the Buddha before he entered Nirvana.

184

Our minds by nature are pure, but because of our ignorance, we created all kinds of sufferings for ourselves. Consequently, we can become free and happy, if we can just shed our ignorance. I urge you to practice diligently like the constant dripping of water that can eventually make a hole in the stone. When we practice this way, we can overcome any hardship.

About the Author

Ven. Pomnyun Sunim* is the founder and the head monk of Jungto Society. He is also an avid social activist, personally leading many projects supporting ecological awareness, human rights and world peace, and eradication of famine, disease and illiteracy. Living up to the motto of Jungto Society, "Pure Mind, Good Friends, and Clean Land," Ven. Pomnyun Sunim has been advocating a new paradigm of civilization in which everyone becomes free and happy with daily spiritual practice, creates a congenial society through active participation in social movements, and protects the environment by adopting simple and earth-friendly way of life.

In his efforts to spread the new paradigm movement, he founded Join Together Society in 1994 to eradicate famine in developing countries; EcoBuddha in 1994 to protect the environment; and Good Friends in 1999 to support human rights, help refugees, and bolster world peace. Also, he established The Peace Foundation, a private research institute, in 2004, to help bring permanent peace, stability, and unification to the Korean peninsula. He has devoted much of his effort to advocating peace and ending famine, disease and illiteracy in many countries around the world including Afghanistan, India, Mongolia,

Myanmar, Philippines, Sri Lanka, and North Korea.

In recognition of his dedication and achievements, Ven. Pomnyun Sunim was presented with the Ramon Magsaysay Award for Peace and International Understanding in September 2002.

In 2011, the Peace Foundation and Jungto Society jointly organized the "Making the World Full of Hope" campaign with the goal of helping people realize their potential and contribute to making the world filled with more hope and happiness. As part of this campaign, Ven. Pomnyun Sunim has given 400 "Hope" lectures in Korea, as well as 70 lectures overseas from 2011 to 2013. This year, he plans to give another 100 "Hope" lectures in various countries around the world.

* Buddhist monks are called "Sunim" in Korea

Books and Commentaries - Korean

A Treatise for Young Buddhist Practitioners

Engaged Buddhism

Buddha - The Life and Philosophy

The Frog Jumped Out of a Well

Commentary on the Heart Sutra

Looking for Happiness in the World - In Search of a Hopeful Paradigm

Commentaries I and II on the Diamond Sutra

Into Worldly Passion, Into the World

New Leadership for Future Generations

Finding Hope

The Way to the Unification of the Korean Peninsula

Buddhism and Environment

Buddhism and Peace

People From Across the Tumen River

I Want to Live a Dignified Life

Following the Footsteps of the Buddha

Open World, Open People

Changes in North Korean Society

From the Korean War to the North and South Talks

Peace of Mind, Compassionate Society

Commentary on Amitayurdhyana Sutra

The Beautiful Harmony of Work and Practice

If You Know the Causes You Have Created, There Is Nothing to Be Unhappy About

Shaken by the Buddha

Sunim, I Feel Unhappy

Today's North Korea, the Tomorrow of North Korea

Books and Commentaries - English

True Happiness

True Freedom

True Wisdom

Books and Commentaries - French

La Famille

Books and Commentaries - Japanese

My Happy Way to Work

Ask, If You Want to Know

お坊さん、どうすれば幸せに結婚できますか?

Books and Commentaries - Chinese

My Happy Way to Work

A Home Full of Laughter

不要害怕彷徨

妈妈课

好婚姻,靠修行

Books and Commentaries _ Thailand

My Happy Way to Work

เดนไปทำงานอยางมความสข

Books and Commentaries - Taiwan

徬徨, 也沒關係

禪師的證婚辭

Books and Commentaries - Viet Nam

Tôi Làm Việc, Tôi Hạnh Phúc

Awards

1998 Kyobo Environmental Education Award, Korea

2000 Manhae Propagation Award, Korea

2002 Ramon Magsaysay Peace and International Understanding Award, Philippines

2006 DMZ(Demilitarized Zone)Peace Prize, Gangwon Province, Korea.

2007 National Reconciliation and Cooperation Award, Korean Council for Reconciliation and Cooperation, Korea

2011 POSCO Chungam Award, POSCO Chungam Foundation

2011 Reunification and Culture Award, Reunification and Culture Research Institute, Segye Daily

Jungto Society, a Community Based on Buddhist Practice

Jungto Society was founded with the aim of building a community of Buddhists who practice together and share the dedication to solve problems that are prevalent in the modern world such as poverty, political and social conflicts, and environmental degradation. While placing emphasis on personal transformation through individual Buddhist practice, Jungto Society has been supporting various social movements such as the raising of ecological awareness; eradication of famine, disease and illiteracy; advocacy of peace and human rights; and the unification of the Korean peninsula.

Ven. Pomnyun Sunim and its members look to the 2,500 year old teachings of the Buddha to find the solutions to modern problems of the world. As Buddhists, its members view the environmental issues and the plight of people in the Third World countries with compassion and wisdom. They have been the active forerunners in various projects to help the people around the world including North Korea and many Third World countries. As of 2014, Jungto Society consists of 102 regional chapters in Korea and 21 overseas chapters including 12 in the United States.

About the Jungto USA Translation Team

The Jungto USA Translation Team is a group of volunteers attending Jungto Society near their homes in various cities across the United States. Currently, there are seven active members volunteering their time and efforts to translate Ven. Pomnyun Sunim's Dharma talks from Korean to English. Although the members vary in profession, gender and age, they share the common experience of having their lives transformed by the wisdom they found in Ven. Pomnyun Sunim's Dharma talks. This team of translators have devoted countless hours to translating this book, because they want to share the wisdom of the Buddha with English speaking readers. English translations of Ven. Pomnyun Sumin's books include True Happiness, True Freedom, and True Wisdom.